Published by Active Education

www.peped.org

First published in 2018

ISBN: 9781976924804

©Active Education Ltd

Cartoons used with permission © Becky Dyer

All images © their respective owners

Links, reviews, news and revision materials available on www.peped.org

www.peped.org website allows students and teachers to explore Philosophy of Religion and Ethics through handouts, film clips, presentations, case studies, extracts, games and academic articles.

Pitched just right, and so much more than a text book, here is a place to engage with critical reflection whatever your level. Marked student essays are also posted.

Contents

'The unexamined life is not worth living' Socrates

About this Guide

The OCR 2016 specification H573 has posed some challenges for teacher and student, and for this reason this guide represents the foundation of a new approach to revision which integrates elements of the Peped project.

- The textbooks have produced their own interpretation of the specification, in the sense of **ADDITIONAL AUTHORS** and ideas, which you don't necessarily need to adopt or follow. They have overlaid an additional discussion of philosophers and philosophical ideas in order to **EVALUATE** the fairly brief content of the specification. So it is essential you understand that you will be examined on knowledge and content alone - and you can use whoever you like to evaluate and criticise this content. **You should download and print out now a hard copy of the relevant pages of the specification**.

- The three papers need to be integrated to produce what is called **SYNOPTIC** insight. This literally means elements of the three papers that can be 'seen together' or linked up. For example, Kant's **MORAL ARGUMENT** (Philosophy of Religion) links and to his ethics which links to **HICK**'s universal **PLURALISM** (Christian Thought) as Hick is greatly inspired by Kant. The Peped website shows additional ways to integrate the three papers and there will be a **REVISION** section accessible for those who have this guide showing you how to increase your synoptic understanding. **Those who have this integrated guide should have a head-start, but you need to supplement it with other ideas and sample answers.**

- Our approach is to teach for **STRUCTURES OF THOUGHT**. These are given by the mind-maps in this guide. Notice these are not free-for-all scatter diagrams but are structures that move from **WORLDVIEW** through to **CONCLUSION**. And the same structure will be there in the website and in the other revision materials - with creative and hopefully enjoyable tasks you can use to test your understanding. You need to run with this concept of structures, and if you do so, I believe your chances of an A grade or A* will be greatly enhanced. They remind us to reason from **WORLDVIEW** and assumptions through to a conclusion that follows. **As you revise, think 'process' rather than 'knowledge'. Knowledge is strengthened by process.**

Peped represents a community of teachers who are talking and testing things all the time, in a great co-operative conversation.

Ultimately we'll only be good philosophers and A* candidates if we have learned to read and **INTERPRET** our culture and make sure our answers are full of relevance as well as crystal clarity and razor-sharp evaluation.

For Peped revision events please go to the website and look under 'Events', and you can meet us in person!

Augustine - Human Nature

Background & Influences

Augustine was influenced in his thought on human nature by:

1. MANICHEES – each person has a good and bad soul. We escape wrong-doing by using our reason and following positive role models.

2. NEOPLATONISM – Plotinus. Good and evil are not distinct realms. Only the Form of the Good exists.

3. BIBLE - St Paul's Letter to the Romans – God's grace was necessary.

At AS and A level, you will need to explain and evaluate Augustine's view on human relationships pre-and post-Fall; Original Sin and its effects on the will and human societies, and God's grace.

Key Terms

- **AKRASIA -** paradox of voluntarily choosing to do something we know is against our best interests.

- **CARITAS -** 'generous love', a love of others and of the virtues.

- **CONCORDIA -** human friendship.

- **CONCUPISCENCE -** uncontrollable desire for physical pleasures and material things.

- **CUPIDITAS** - 'selfish love', a love of worldly things and of selfish desires.

- **DOCTRINE** - means 'teaching'. The official teaching of the Roman Catholic Church.

- **ECCLESIA** - heavenly society, in contrast with earthly society.

- **GRACE** - theologically, God's free and unearned love for humankind, embodied in the sacrifice of Jesus on the cross.

- **MANICHEES** - humans have two souls. One desires God, the other desires evil. Evil is not caused by God, but by a lower power. The body is evil and sinful.

- **NEOPLATONISM** - influenced by Plato; the body belongs to the realm of flesh and is necessarily imperfect.

- **ONTOLOGICAL** - the being or nature of existence.

- **OPTIMISTIC VIEW OF HUMAN NATURE** - humans are only immoral because of poor education or psychological fault.

- **ORIGINAL SIN** - Christian belief that despite being made in God's image the human condition means we cannot reach this state.

- **PELAGIANS** - Christians who believed humans could overcome personal sin with free will. No universal guilt.

- **POST-LAPSARIAN** - the world after the fall of Adam and Eve.

- **SUMMUM BONUM** - he highest, most supreme good.

- **THE FALL** - the biblical event in which Adam and Eve disobeyed God's command and ate the fruit from the forbidden tree in the Garden of Eden.

Structure of Thought

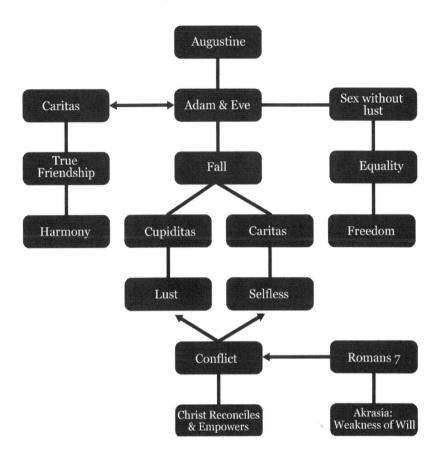

Human Relationships Pre and Post-Fall

The **ORIGINAL SIN** of Adam and Eve ruined the relationship humankind could have had with God.

Augustine teaches that this '**ORIGINAL SIN**' passes on through generations **SEMINALLY** (by sperm), making human nature flawed. However, Jesus' death on the cross was seen as a **SACRIFICE**, paying the price of sin, meaning Christians could be saved through God's **GRACE**.

Christian tradition understands humanity in terms of its relationship with God. This is threefold:

1. Humans are **CREATED** by God.

2. Humans are **FALLEN** in nature.

3. Humans can be **REDEEMED** (bought back by a sacrifice).

Pre-Fall

The shared nature of **IMAGO DEI** means humans can all be seen to be equal. This has soemtimes been seen as **EQUALLY RATIONAL**, but at other times women are seen as **COMPLEMENTARY** - but less rational (**AQUINAS**).

In **GENESIS** the second account of creation shows humans as **SPECIAL** in God's creation but simultaneously part of the natural world. God breathes life into man. God animates man - different to **PLATO'S** notion of the soul trapped by the body.

Once created, humans are not programmed to act in a certain way. They have a set of rules to follow e.g. multiply, be stewards, do not eat from the forbidden tree. They have potential to be both obedient and disobedient – made with **FREE CHOICE** and made perfectly.

Humans were made with a **DUTY OF OBEDIENCE** to God's demands and existed harmoniously, observing their duties to other living creatures.

The state of perfection **PRE-FALL** meant that the human will, the body, and reason cooperated with each other entirely. In their **SEXUAL** expression **AUGUSTINE** argues that pre-Fall Adam and Eve had perfect **SELF-CONTROL**.

Humans are naturally sociable and friendship is the highest form of this. **CONCORDIA** is used to describe Adam and Eve's relationship pre-**FALL**. Adam and Eve were not just living together, but were living in a state of the very best of all possible **HARMONIOUS** human relationships.

Post-Fall

The will can be driven by **CUPIDITAS** (self-love typified by **LUST** or **CARITAS** (selfless-love or benevolence).

After the first free decision to disobey, Adam and Eve became aware of their sexual bodies. Through **REASON** the will knows what is good but is often motivated by **CONCUPISCENCE** (sexual lust) rather than by goodness. Concupiscence can distract from God and break up friendship.

Post-Fall, the will became in conflict with itself and could lead to freely choosing what we know to go against our best interests. This is known as **AKRASIA** (weakness of will).

Augustine used his own example of a beautiful, chaste woman – **CONTINENCE**. Not even she could convince Augustine to embrace celibacy – **"Lord, make me chaste, but not yet!"**.

The battle with sin cannot be won without turning to Christ, as shown in Paul's Letter to the **ROMANS,** (chapter 7) and the extracts from **CONFESSIONS**.

SYNOPTIC point: in the Ethics paper, Freud's theory of **CONSCIENCE** suggests a struggle between the **PASSIONS** of the **ID** and the restraint of the **SUPEREGO**.

Original Sin - Effects on the Human Will & Society

Augustine and Pelagius

AUGUSTINE sees sin as an **ONTOLOGICAL CONDITION** of Human Existence. We might appear **VIRTUOUS**, but no one is truly good. Sin was transmitted by **SEXUAL INTERCOURSE**.

PELAGIUS argues that while Adam set a poor example, it was not the one that we had to follow and we could, if we tried, live morally.

Augustine disagreed with Pelagius - human efforts alone were not enough – we need God's **GRACE** and **CHRIST**. Paul said much the same "the things I do not want are the things I do' (**ROMANS 7**). Paul sees human beings as **SLAVES** to sin.

The inherited **ORIGINAL SIN** causes human selfishness and a lack of free will; plus a lack of stability and corruption in all human societies. **CUPIDITAS** (selfish desire) has won over **CARITAS** (the harmonious love of Eden) and the human soul is now in **CONFLICT.**

Human Selfishness & Free Will

The **FALL** left the will divided. Paul's Letter to the **ROMANS** described Paul's struggle between his **SELFISH DESIRES** and his **SPIRITUAL INCLINATIONS**, (see Romans 7).

Paul speaks of Christians as 'forgiven sinners' through their faith and this partially explains how Christians still behave wrongly even after accepting salvation. Paul implies that the release from all sin will come with death of the body.

SEXUAL LUSTS are evidence of sinful **CUPIDITAS**. **AUGUSTINE** said that even within marriage, a couple should take a vow of **CELIBACY** once they had had enough children. People should live plainly and simply to devote themselves to God.

In '**On the Good of Marriage**' - the physical delight of sex in marriage should be distinguished from **LIBIDO** (misuse of lustful impulse). It is 'pardonable' to enjoy sex without the intention of procreation. Like **ARISTOTLE** and **PAUL**, he stressed **'**mutual **OBLIGATION'.**

In '**On Free Will**' Augustine suggests free will allows us to use reason to aspire to the Good (human flourishing) by living virtuously. This is **PLATONIC**.

However, human reason cannot overcome the punishments of the Fall. Sin is **INVOLUNTARY** and we cannot help but fall into wrong-doing. We prefer to do wrong because our souls are 'chained' by sin. Neither living **ASCETICALLY** (nun/ monk) or opting for a **CHASTE** life could enable the will to be free and strong enough to resist **CONCUPISCENCE** in its various forms.

Lack of Stability & Corruption in Human Societies

A forceful political **AUTHORITY** was needed to help society function.

The Bible teaches that humans are appointed to rule over other species, but not each other. **PRE-FALL**, leaders in society were **SHEPHERDS** not kings (Augustine, City of God).

'Earthly peace' is a material and not a spiritual aim. **EARTHLY PEACE** is the best sort of life sinful people can aim for, but even this is **CORRUPTED**. The measures needed for earthy peace (e.g. self-restraint) are only necessary because of the Fall.

Commitment to the common good is a consequence of sinful human nature and not, as **AQUINAS** would say, a **MORAL VIRTUE**. We are '**PILGRIMS** in a foreign land' – we need to live as earthly people out of necessity; but should keep focused on the heavenly destination, the **'CITY OF GOD'**.

This '**HEAVENLY SOCIETY** is called **ECCLESIA** and is 'perfect living'. Heavenly society is known only through death and the **GRACE** of God and is poorly and partially reflected in the **EARTHLY** society.

God's Grace

AUGUSTINE argued that the rebellious will and **SIN** could only be overcome by God's grace (his free and generous gifts), made possible through Jesus' sacrifice. Only then can the supreme good (**SUMMUM BONUM**) be achieved.

Augustine's teaching on God's grace laid the foundation for Catholic confession – the Sacrament of **RECONCILIATION**.

The Christian doctrine of **ELECTION** teaches that salvation is possible because

God chooses to redeem (literally 'buy back' from the slave market) humans first. God has elected those He knows will answer His love and be restored to paradise. The elected are assisted by the **HOLY SPIRIT.**

Augustine's view contradicts one New Testament suggestion that 'all' are saved – unless this means that God saves across races and cultures (see 2 Peter 3:9).

JOHN 3 ('Jesus said; unless a person is born again of **WATER** and the Spirit they cannot enter the Kingdom of God') led Augustine to believe that heaven could not be reached by anyone deliberately denying baptism. **UNBAPTISED** babies could be condemned to hell. This is not as a result of choice – infants do not 'choose' to deny baptism.

Faith in God's love and an acknowledgement of the failings of human nature are essential on the path to **EUDAIMONIA** - "unless you believe, you will not understand" (Isaiah 7:9).

John 3 showed Augustine that **FAITH** and **BAPTISM** together were needed as human nature is **ONTOLOGICALLY** flawed (flawed in its very essence).

God's **GRACE** is understood as:

- God's **LOVE** and **MERCY**; that He is capable of reaching the heart and will of a person and can give moral guidance to the lives of Christians; something that cannot be deserved by any human on their own merit.

- The quality that enables a person's soul to **RECOGNISE** when it has offended God and when it should praise God.

- Capable of **TRANSFORMING** the human will so that it is capable of obeying God.

- Capable of **OVERCOMING** human pride and can calm the soul with forgiveness and hope.

- **VISIBLE** in Christ's sacrifice and in the gift of the Holy Spirit working in the Church.

MNEMONIC: Lovely Mary Really Transformed Our Vase

Happiness in this earthly life is temporary. Plato's **FORM OF THE GOOD** is similar to **AUGUSTINE**'s understanding of God's goodness in Christianity. The **SUMMUM BONUM** is a state of eternal happiness. It cannot be earned and is the highest goal one can aim for – achievable only through God's grace.

Strengths

1. Close to the reality that people often find themselves **TEMPTED** by material goods, yet wanting to do right.

2. **AUGUSTINE** draws attention to the dangers of uncontrolled sexual behaviour – see how societies restrict it. Recognising human imperfection might lead to more moral progress.

3. The **PELAGIAN** belief that human effort could bring about perfection was optimistic and doomed to fail. Augustine's teaching of our imperfect natures allows us to have genuine hope in God's grace.

4. The **BODY** and human **REASON** can be in tension with the body being willing, but the will not so. This supports the view that sex must have been under the control of the human will pre-Fall. Sex did not come about because of **the Fall**; but rather, was affected by it.

5. Other schools of thought suggest a **SINGLE** human nature. E.g. Buddhism

– human nature is characterised by the impermanency of all things and suffering because of attachment and desires. Evolutionary biology suggests the single human nature that is driven by survival instinct.

Weaknesses

1. **ORIGINAL SIN** as 'ontologically present' is difficult to reconcile with belief in a benevolent God. Human nature is not fundamentally corrupt! **ROUSSEAU** argued that humans are, by nature, good and inclined to defend the weak and work for a better society. Rousseau and Locke later asserted the 'blank state' (**'TABULA RASA'**). We are born with – neither a good nor evil state, but readiness to make free choices..

2. **SARTRE**, an **EXISTENTIALIST**, suggests we have the freedom to create our own nature – rather than being born condemned.

3. **PREDESTINATION**/ Election – if our fates are already decided, what responsibility can we have for our moral actions? With no real freedom, what incentive do we have to become better?

4. Richard **DAWKINS** - while the Christian concept of 'original sin' does not wholly contradict evolutionary biology, the idea that human nature could be restored through the death of Jesus is sado-masochistic!

5. **FREUD** (1856-1939) – one of the founders of psychoanalysis – wrote that sex is an important and natural aspect of human development; whereas **Augustine's** link between sex and transmission of sin makes sex only necessary for reproduction. Sex can transmit human disorders but sin is not one of these! Rather than a product of sexual intercourse, sin is a product of our environment (family, religion, education, or lack thereof). Augustine

fails to acknowledge the natural enjoyment of sex within marriage.

6. Steven **PINKER** (psychologist) supports **DAWKINS**. God's Grace is not needed as our actions as rational, autonomous beings can succeed and allow us responsibility.

Possible Exam Questions

1. Assess the view that Augustine's teaching on human nature is too pessimistic.

2. Critically assess the view that Christian teaching on human nature can only make sense if the Fall did actually happen.

3. "Augustine's teaching on human nature is more harmful than helpful". Discuss.

4. How convincing is Augustine's teaching about the Fall and Original Sin?

5. Critically assess Augustine's analysis of human sexual nature.

Key Quotes

"For they would not have arrived at the evil act if an evil will had not preceded it". (Augustine, city of God).

"I do not understand what I do. For what I want to do I do not do, but what I hate I do". (St. Paul's Letter to the Romans)

"In vain did I delight in Your law after the inner man, when another law in my members warred against the law of my mind." (Augustine, Confessions).

"No one can enter the kingdom of God unless they are born of water and the Spirit". (John 3)

"Whoever believes in him is not condemned, but whoever does not believe stands condemned already." (John 3)

"What kind of ethical philosophy is it that condemns every child, even before it is born, to inherit the sin of a remote ancestor?" (Richard Dawkins, God Delusion)

Death and the Afterlife

Background & Influences

Jesus' teachings rooted in **JEWISH TRADITION** and **ESCHATOLOGY** (teaching on the end-times) of his time. Influenced by the teaching of the **PHARISEES** who were influenced by **GREEK** ideas of the soul and immortality.

Jesus taught his life was a **SACRIFICE** for sin and his death would bring about a **NEW KINGDOM**.

Some believed the 'new Kingdom' to be **IMMINENT** (about to happen). Different beliefs about the Kingdom of God include whether it is **an actual place, a spiritual state, or a symbol of moral life.**

You will need to show knowledge and evaluation of Christian teaching on Heaven, Hell, and Purgatory, and Christian teaching on Election.

Key Terms

- **ESCHATOLOGY** - discussion of the end-times, including battle between good and evil and God's judgement of the world.

- **PHARISEES** - influential religious leaders at the time of Jesus. Differed to other traditional Jews at the time (e.g. Sadducees) because the Pharisees did believe in angels and bodily resurrection.

- **PAROUSIA** - Greek for 'arrival'. Christ's 'second coming'.

- **KINGDOM OF GOD** - God's rule in this world and the next.

- **HADES** and **GEHENNA**: Hades – for departed spirits awaiting judgement; Gehenna - a symbol for eternal punishment of the wicked.

- **MARANATHA** - Aramaic – 'O Lord, come!' 1 Cor 16:22 (once in NT).

- **PURGATORY** - where those who have died in a state of grace continue to seek forgiveness and receive punishment awaiting Final Judgement.

- **MORTAL SIN** - sin deliberately in defiance of God's law.

- **VENIAL SIN** - errors of judgement, can be forgiven.

- **BEATIFIC VISION** - final and perfect human state of everlasting happiness and knowledge of God.

- **PREDESTINATION** - Christian teaching that God chooses and guides some people to eternal salvation.

- **DOUBLE PREDESTINATION** - God elects the righteous for Heaven and condemns sinners to Hell - as in **CALVIN**'s teaching.

- **WESTMINSTER CONFESSION OF FAITH** - 1646, sets out principle beliefs of Reformed Christianity.

- **SINGLE PREDESTINATION** - God predestines some to heaven but the wicked elect Hell for themselves. Official **CATHOLIC** teaching.

Structure of Thought

Christian Teaching on Heaven, Hell and Purgatory

1. Heaven, hell, and purgatory as **ACTUAL PLACES**.

2. Heaven, hell, and purgatory as not places, but **SPIRITUAL STATES** that a person experiences as part of their spiritual journey after death.

3. Heaven, hell, and purgatory as **SYMBOLS** of a person's spiritual and moral life on earth and not places or states after death.

Ideas about the Kingdom Taught by Jesus

1. A present moral and spiritual state. A call for moral and spiritual reform now. Jesus' healing miracles seem to fulfil prophecies of Isaiah and Jesus presents the Kingdom of God as if it has already begun. This 'nowness' is seen in his parables and examples of how to reach out to the lowly.

2. A future redeemed state. Made possible through Jesus' death and resurrection.

3. A place of punishment and justice. Where the wicked will suffer and those who suffered will prosper. - **GEHENNA** - a place of **EVERLASTING FIRE** (Matthew 25 - Parable of the Sheep & Goats).

Problems

1. PAROUSIA seems delayed. One of the earliest prayers recorded is for the Parousia – **MARANATHA** prayer (1 Corinthians 16:22, 'Come Lord Jesus!').

Jesus emphasises the mystery surrounding this date.

2. WHERE is this new Kingdom? On earth or in heaven (or both)?

3. FINAL JUDGEMENT v INDIVIDUAL – which is more important? Rich man and Lazarus implies judgement is immediate (Luke 16:13-31). Others suggest it happens at the end-time.

4. PURGATORY is not a term used in the New Testament. Arose out of fairness to allow people time to prepare for God's final judgement and as a result of ambiguity surrounding personal and final judgement.

Eschatological Teaching

1. **PAROUSIA** (second coming of Christ)

2. **RESURRECTION** (at the last day a 'trumpet will sound', 1 Cor. 15)

3. **JUDGEMENT** (Matthew 25 - sheep and goats separated)

Hell - Different Ideas

SPIRITUAL STATE: Origen (184-253 AD) – a person's interior anguish separated from God, where "each sinner kindles his own fire ...and our own vices from its fuel" (Cited in Wilcockson & Campbell, 2016, p. 273).

CONSCIENCE: Gregory of Nyssa (335-395 AD) – a guilty conscience when before Christ leads to judgement and torture of Hell.

DANTE (1265-1321): Hell is antithesis to Heaven – "through me the way into the woeful city, through me the way to eternal pain...abandon every hope, ye that enter" (Dante Divine Comedy cited in Wilcockson & Campbell, 2016:274).

SYMBOL OF ALIENATION: Paul Tillich (1886-1965) – hell-type language has a place. Traditional metaphors are reinterpreted as spiritual and psychological descriptions of human alienation: "heaven and hell must be taken seriously as metaphors for the polar ultimates in the experience of the divine" (Tillich, P, Systematic theology III, 1964, p. 446, cited in Wilcockson & Campbell, 2016:275).

HELL AS ETERNAL SEPARATION: Catholic teaching – Hell is real eternal for those who have committed mortal sins.

Purgatory

1. A **CATHOLIC** way of extending the opportunity for repentance beyond this life, even though there is no clear representation of this in the New Testament, just one hint **1 PETER 3:19**. "When made alive, Jesus went to preach to the spirits in prison".

2. Foretaste of Heaven and Hell – **AMBROSE** (340 -397 AD).

3. Probationary school – **ORIGEN**.

4. Redemption of the whole of creation – **GREGORY** of Nyssa – purgatory has a **PURIFYING PURPOSE** for all people to help God complete his purpose of restoring all creation.

Dante's Vision

- For souls who believed in Christ and repented before death; a place for positive **PURGING** since one cannot sin in purgatory.

- The soul ascends terrains of mountain, the goal of which is **BEATIFIC VISION**. Soul is driven by love and later on, reason. An allegory for how life should be lived on earth too with its various temptations before the goal of salvation.

Catholic Teaching on Purgatory

- Ideas of **CLEANSING** of sins by fires implies that forgiveness is possible in this and in the next life.

- A **STAGE** in the soul's journey to salvation.

- Prayers for the dead pre-dates Christianity – **JUDAS MACCAAEUS** (2nd C BC) – prayed that the souls of the dead should be freed from sin. Sale of **INDULGENCES** (masses said for the dead) one reason for **REFORMATION** protest in the sixteenth century.

- St John **CHRYSOSTOM** writes:

"All who die in God's grace and friendship, but still imperfectly purified, are indeed assured of their eternal salvation; but after death they undergo purification, so as to achieve the holiness necessary to enter the joy of heaven". St John Chrysostom

Hick - The Intermediary State

The majority of Protestants reject **PURGATORY** on the grounds of lack of Biblical evidence.

A minority of **LIBERAL PROTESTANTS** are persuaded of the continued journey of the soul after death.

JOHN HICK says that the gap between our imperfection at the end of this life, and the state of perfection is a **SOUL-MAKING** process begun on Earth.

Heaven

This has a number of meanings. The **RESTORATION** of the whole of creation, not just the individual's relationship with God.

DANTE – Heaven is beyond words. Rational soul strives for ultimate good and Divine harmony. God as source of love and governor of universe is experienced.

CATHOLIC TEACHING – Heaven is a "state of supreme, definitive happiness" (Cited in Wilcockson & Campbell, 2016, p. 278). God is wholly revealed in **BEATIFIC VISION**. A community of immortal souls in communion with Christ and obedient.

Election - Who Will Be Saved?

Limited Election

• Only a few Christians will be saved

• **'LIMITED ATONEMENT'** – Christ died only for the sins of the Elect

Unlimited Election

• All people called to salvation, not all are saved

• **'UNLIMITED ATONEMENT'** – Christ died for the sins of the whole world

Universalist Belief (Apokatastasis - Restoration)

• All people will be saved - required by God's goodness and love

- A requirement of human free will – we should all be able to reach salvation

- Upbringing should not exclude people from reconciliation with God

JOHN HICK – The God preached about by Jesus is not one who excludes. Jesus' resurrection is a triumph over death, not eternal damnation.

KARL BARTH - CALVINIST and not strictly universalist but helpful. God is both elected and elector and it is not for humans to speculate on the mystery of salvation.

Predestination

Election and Predestination

AUGUSTINE argued that salvation is only possible because of God's grace. God's grace is unprompted but **FREELY GIVEN.** God calls all to salvation but knows from the beginning that only some are eligible for a place in Heaven (**ELECT**).

Some are not capable of receiving God's grace and are predestined for Hell (**PERDITION**).

Single and Double Predestination

- **SINGLE**: God elects only those for Heaven

- **DOUBLE**: God elects people for both Heaven and Hell.

- **ANTELAPSARIAN DECREE**: God decreed the elect at the moment of creation, pre-Fall (literally **ANTE** - before **LAPSARIAN,** the lapse).

- **POSTLAPSARIAN DECREE:** God decreed the elect post-Fall.

Calvin

Developing ideas in Paul's letter to the Ephesians, Calvin argued God **FOREKNOWS** what will happen but His will is hidden. Calvin believed both saved and damned are **PREDESTINED** from the beginning of time. This is **DOUBLE PREDESTINATION.**

As Human knowledge is **LIMITED**, God's revelation takes this into account. **GOD WILLS** his grace and mercy for all kinds of people.

Even if God has chosen particular individuals, **CHRISTIAN DUTY** is to spread God's words to all kinds of people. Both the **ELECT** and the **NON-ELECT** have a duty to act morally.

Thomas Aquinas and Catholicism

AQUINAS argued the Fall did not wipe out human freedom. THE Catholic Church – argues for **SINGLE** predestination of the saved - damned get to hell by choice.

"God predestines no one to go to Hell; for this, a wilful turning away from God (a mortal sin) is necessary, and persistence in it until the end" (Catechism of the Catholic Church para. 1037).

Parable of Sheep & Goats (Matthew 25)

- **REVERSAL of expectation.** 'Righteous' would have been thought to have meant those who observed Jewish law. Jesus teaches that religious observance is not enough to earn a place in God's Kingdom. One must pursue justice for the marginalised without thinking of heavenly reward.

- **REWARD** is for **ALL** who pursue justice, not just Christians. The God of love rewards all of good will.

- **REVELATION** of Jesus' own ministry of healing and serving the oppressed is reflected in his list of acts that would be rewarded.

- **CHALLENGE** to traditional teaching that you are only obligated to help those in the same social and religious group as yourself. "Just as you did to one of the least of these who are members of my family, you did it to me" (Matthew 25:40).

Possible Exam Questions

1. To what extent can belief in the existence of purgatory be justified?

2. "Heaven is not a place but a state of mind." Discuss.

3. "Without the reward of Heaven Christians would not behave well." Discuss.

4. To what extent is the Parable of the Sheep and the Goats in Matthew 25 only about Heaven and Hell?

5. Assess the view that there is no last judgement; each person is judged by God at the moment of their death.

6. "Purgatory is a vital Christian teaching about the afterlife." Discuss.

Key Quotes

"The time is fulfilled, and the kingdom of God is near" (Mark 1:14)

"But if it is by the finger of God that I cast out the demons, then the kingdom of God has come to you" (Luke 11:20).

"Then the eyes of the blind shall be opened, and the ears of the deaf unstopped; then the lame shall leap like a deer, the tongue of the speechless sing for joy" (Isaiah 35:5-6).

"Anyone whose name was not found written in the book of life was thrown into the lake of fire" (Revelation 20:15).

"But about that day and hour no one knows, neither the angels of heaven, nor the Son, but only the Father" (Matthew 24:36).

"If what has been built on the foundation survives, the builder will receive a reward. If the work is burned the builder will suffer loss; the builder will be saved, but only as through fire" (1 Corinthians 3:14-15).

"God has not rejected his people whom he foreknew" (Romans 11:2).

"This is good, and is acceptable in the sight of God our Saviour, who desires all men to be saved and come to the knowledge of truth" (1 Timothy 2:4).

"All who die in God's grace and friendship, but still imperfectly purified, are indeed assured of their eternal salvation; but after death they undergo purification, so as to achieve the holiness necessary to enter the joy of

heaven." *(Catechism 1030)*

"The Church gives the name Purgatory to this final purification of the elect, which is entirely different from the punishment of the damned. The tradition of the Church, by reference to certain texts of Scripture, speaks of a cleansing fire". (Catechism 1031)

Knowledge of God

Background & Influences

NATURAL THEOLOGY is concerned with demonstrating God's existence. Some have assumed God's existence to be logically true. God revealed in the natural world seems removed from Biblical ideas of God as love.

REVEALED THEOLOGY suggests that God allows himself to be known in a special way e.g. in Jesus Christ or the example of the Prophet Muhammad (PBUH).

Problem: God is uniquely different to any other object. Natural theology would have to accept this. Revealed theology seems to neglect reason.

What is 'true knowledge'?

1. **Incorrigible facts** (verifiable)

2. **Wisdom** – understanding life and what gives it value

3. **Knowledge** of God as the source of life

At A level, you will need to show understanding and evaluation of natural knowledge of God's existence as an innate human sense of the Divine, and as seen in the order of Creation; and revealed knowledge of God's existence through faith and God's grace, and in Jesus Christ.

Key Terms

- **NATURAL THEOLOGY** - God can be known through reason and observation of the natural world.

- **REVEALED THEOLOGY** - God can only be known when he lets himself be known e.g. through prophets, scripture, prayer.

- **SENSUS DIVINITATIS** - Latin used by Calvin to mean a 'sense of God'.

- **DUPLEX COGNITIO DOMINI** - 'two-fold knowledge of God' – Calvin's distinction of knowing God as Creator and as Redeemer.

- **ARGUMENT FROM DESIGN** - we must infer a designer (God) of the universe from the universe's complexities.

- **PRINCIPLE OF ACCOMMODATION** - God reveals himself through creation in ways that limited human minds can best understand.

- **SI INTEGER STETISSET ADAM** - Latin used by Calvin meaning 'if Adam had remained upright' – referring to the Fall.

- **TRINITARIAN VIEW OF GOD** - central to the Christian teaching that God is one but reveals Himself as three 'persons': Father, son, Holy Spirit.

- **IMMANENCE** - 'being part of' – refers to God's participation in all aspects of the world and universe.

- **ATHEOLOGICAL OBJECTOR** - term used by Plantinga to refer to those who reject all theological claims.

- **FIDEISM** - Revelation is essential for the human mind to know anything certain about the existence of God or nature.

Structure of Thought

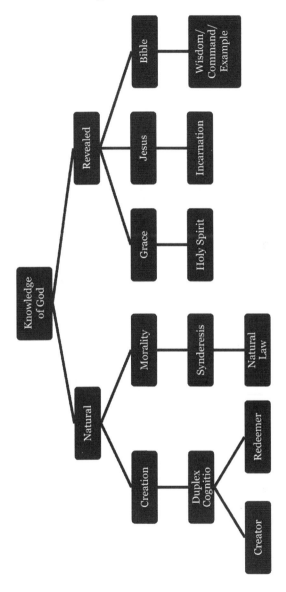

Natural Knowledge of God's Existence as an Innate Sense of the Divine

Sensus Divinitatis

As all humans are made in God's **IMAGE** - they have an inbuilt capacity and desire to know God, including:

- Human **OPENNESS** to beauty and goodness as aspects of God

- Human **INTELLECTUAL** ability to reflect on and recognise God's existence

Both **CALVIN** and the **CATECHISM** of the Catholic Church agree that knowledge of God is **INNATE** (we are born with it).

CALVIN called this innate knowledge of God **SENSUS DIVINITATIS**.

SEMEN RELIGIONIS – seed of religion – human inclination to carry out religious practices e.g. rituals and prayer.

Innate Knowledge

- **UNKNOWN GOD – Acts 17:16-34** – Paul tries to convince Athenians they are worshipping the true God, even if they do not know this.

- **UNIVERSAL CONSENT – Cicero, Calvin** – so many people believe in a God/ gods that there **MUST** exist a God/god!

- **HUMANS ARE RELIGIOUS** – religious rituals and meditations are so universal that "**one may well call man a religious being**" (Catechism 28).

Sense of Beauty & Moral Goodness

The foundations of knowledge of God in Protestant and Catholic Christianity.

- **NATURAL LAW** – particularly Catholicism – all humans have an innate awareness of justice and fairness, even if ill-informed. Aquinas calls this innate orientation to the good **SYNDERESIS**. ~ Do good avoid evil.

- **CONSCIENCE** – particularly important to Calvin's ideas about knowledge of God. Conscience is God-given to humans made **IMAGO DEI** with 'Joint knowledge' between us and God. God's presence gives us the sense of moral judgement within us.

Human Intellectual Ability to Reflect on & Recognise God's Existence

Seen in example of **Thomas Aquinas' FIVE WAYS** - God as **UNCAUSED CAUSER** who sustains all things.

Best knowledge we have here is that God exists differently to other beings.

Consider: how can we be **SURE** that this is God?

Natural Knowledge in the Order of Creation

- The idea that what can be known of God can be seen in the apparent design and purpose of nature

- **CALVIN – duplex cognitio Domini** – two-fold knowledge of God as **CREATOR** and as **REDEEMER**.

- The **ORDER** and **DESIGN** in the universe are strong sources of revelation.

- **PRINCIPLE OF ACCOMMODATION** – Calvin's explanation that human minds are finite and therefore cannot know God through **REASON** alone. Hence, God manifests himself through creation.

- What we know of God through creation is "a sort of **MIRROR** in which we can contemplate God, who is otherwise invisible" (John Calvin: Institutes I.V. 1).

Purpose

- William **PALEY** – watch analogy; God as infinitely powerful maker.

- Challenge- nature seems more cruel than beautiful. Darwin's challenge of evolution too.

- **PROCESS THEOLOGY** developed in response to challenges to Paley's argument and influenced by the principle of **QUANTUM UNCERTAINTY**. Proposes that God works **WITH** the natural processes, not separate to them. Each individual moment is an end in itself – the universe as a whole is not working towards a particular end.   Moltmann.

- **GOD IS KNOWABLE** – in contrast with ideas of classical theology. God loves and suffers with creation, helping each aspect to achieve its potential. God's participation in nature is revealed in every moment of creation. Process theology - there is no clear difference between natural and revealed theology.

Revealed Knowledge of God's Existence

As humans are sinful and have finite minds, natural knowledge is not sufficient to gain full knowledge of God; knowledge of God is possible through:

- **FAITH** - "Happy are those that do not see yet believe". (John 20:29)

- **GRACE** - as God's gift of knowledge of himself through the Holy Spirit

The Fall and Human Finiteness

The **FALL** of humanity has been overlooked in thinking about how we can come to know God, if at all.

- *Si integer stetisset Adam* (if Adam had not sinned) – everyone would have known God (**CALVIN'S** view).

- Knowledge of God the **REDEEMER**, mediated through Christ is part of our **REGENERATION** (of being 'born again').

- **CATHOLIC** – the Fall confused human desire for God but did not cut them off from knowledge of God completely – seen through "religious ignorance or indifference" (Catechism para. 29).

Faith

- Faith needs some **REASON** for it not to be meaningless or random.

- **CATHOLIC** – faith is not independent to reason.

- **AQUINAS** – distinguished between **formed** and **unformed** faith.

- **FORMED FAITH** - faith that wills to accept what it can believe through the intellect. Takes time and effort e.g. belief in resurrection based on witness accounts.

- **UNFORMED FAITH** - may find intellectual reasons why to believe e.g. in afterlife BUT cannot accept as truth.

- **CALVIN** – faith is firm and certain knowledge and a willingness to believe.

Aquinas - ratio, - right reasoning
Do you avoid evil.

- **FIRM AND CERTAIN KNOWLEDGE** - Christ is direct object of faith. Firm knowledge only possible revealed through Christ and by the Holy Spirit.

- **WILLINGNESS TO BELIEVE** - an emotional and spiritual experience of assurance – given to anyone willing to accept it.

Grace

- **CATHOLIC** and **CALVINIST** teaching both agree that faith alone is not enough to know God. God's grace completes the relationship.

- **AQUINAS** – faith can only be justified by grace through the Holy Spirit.

- **CALVIN** – the Holy Spirit is a gift repairing the damage caused by Original Sin. *election of the Jew.*

Revealed Knowledge of God's Existence in Jesus Christ

Full and perfect knowledge of God is revealed in the person of Jesus Christ and through:

- The life of the **CHURCH**

- The **BIBLE**

Bible should be read from a **TRINITARIAN** perspective: God as **FATHER** (God spoke **DIRECTLY** by the **PROPHETS**); God as Christ the **MEDIATOR** (clarity and fulfilment to God's promises); **HOLY SPIRIT** (Christians inspired).

CALVIN – Christ is mediator and mirror of God.

CATHOLIC – agrees but adds that the significance should not end with Christ but should continue with our faith, re-thinking God's revelation continuously.

Consider: can God be known by non-Christians?

The Bible and the Life of the Church

- For traditional Catholics and Protestants, *"God is the author of sacred Scripture…[and its words are] the speech of God as it is put down in writing under the breath of the Holy Spirit"* (Catechism, 105).

- Christianity cannot be 'reduced' to the Bible - which is **INSPIRED** not **DICTATED** (contrast with the Qur'an - dictated by angel Gabriel).

- **CALVIN** – the Bible, read from the perspective of Jesus Christ - as revealer of God the Redeemer; prepared for in the Old Testament and culminates in the events of the New Testament.

- Bible is a significant source for knowledge of God, even for those adopting an approach of **NATURAL THEOLOGY** who might say the Bible reveals early experiences people had of God (Hebrew, as recorded in the **OLD TESTAMENT**) and to the early Christian communities.

- Knowledge of God revealed is **PERSONAL** and **COLLECTIVE**.

"In you, O Lord, I take refuge; let me never be put to shame…incline your ear to me and save me" (Psalm 71:1-2).

Natural theology – design/Cosmos
Innate ability,
Revelation – immediate/mediate revelation.
Faith + God's grace.
Revelation through the Bible –
Acts 17:16 - 34.

Q. WHAT IS THE BARTH/BRUNNER DEBATE?

Brunner

- God's **general revelation** in nature allows humans to become aware of God's commands and the sinful state of humankind.

- **Jesus Christ** reveals **redemption**. Natural theology has limited purpose.

- **Imago Dei** – God's image in humans was materially but not spiritually destroyed in the Fall but not spiritually. This spiritual level allows God to address humans.

- **General revelation** – Innately sinful humans are incapable of seeing God's revelation of his nature through nature – they can know God exists but it remains a **point of contact**, no more.

- **True knowledge** – Faith in Christ is necessary for true knowledge of God.

- **Conscience** – plus guilt bring humans to awareness of God's law.

MNEMONIC: Isabella Gave Temi Cookies

Barth

- There are no points of contact in nature – human nature is absolutely corrupted by the Fall.

- Only God can choose to reveal himself to sinful humans.

Three disagreements with Brunner's interpretation of Calvin:

1. Formal self (spiritual self) cannot inform the **material (physical)**

self of God's existence. Brunner underestimates the corruption of the material self.

2. No points of contact. Nature, conscience and guilt are results of God's grace – they do not provide the points of contact themselves!

3. Order of creation. Perception of order in nature should not be basis for morality. God's moral commands are different to any natural laws. We only see order in creation after it is revealed to us through faith and the Bible.

Possible Exam Questions

1. Discuss critically the view that Christians can discover truths about God using human reason.

2. "Faith is all that is necessary to gain knowledge of God." Discuss.

3. "God can be known because the world is so well designed." Discuss.

4. Critically assess the view that the Bible is the only way of knowing God.

5. "Everyone has an innate knowledge of God's existence." Discuss.

6. To what extent is faith in God rational?

Key Quotes

"The desire for God is written in the human heart" (Catechism of the Catholic Church para. 27).

"No-one can look upon himself without immediately tuning his thoughts to the contemplation of God, in whom he 'lives and moves' (Acts 17:28)" (John Calvin: Institutes I.I.1).

"For what can be known about God is plain to them, because God has shown it to them" (Romans 1:19-20).

"In this ruin of mankind no one now experiences God...until Christ the Mediator comes forward to reconcile him to us". (John Calvin: Institutes I.II. 1).

"Faith is the great cop-out, the great excuse to evade the need to think and evaluate experience" (Richard Dawkins (Edinburgh International Science Festival, April 1992) cited in Wilcockson & Campbell, 2016, p. 293).

"Yet even if Revelation is already complete, it has not been completely explicit; it remains for Christian faith gradually to grasp its full significance over the course of the centuries." (Catechism para. 66).

"The heavens are telling the glory of God; and the firmament proclaims his handiwork" (Psalm 19:1).

"Yet, in the first place, wherever you cast your eyes, there is no spot in the universe wherein you cannot discern at least some sparks of his glory" (John

Calvin: Institutes I.V.1).

"Both experience and history point to a God who acts not by coercing but by evoking the response of his creatures." (Ian G. Barbour: Issues in Science and Religion (1966:463).

Person of Jesus Christ

Background & Influences

Jesus' influence as an authority comes from his teachings, his example, and his relationship with God. Jesus' moral teachings have allowed him to have authority, even for non-Christians.

As teacher of **WISDOM** (and Rabbi), Jesus developed Jewish ethics; as **LIBERATOR**, he challenged political and religious authorities; and as **SON OF GOD**, Jesus came to bring salvation and to carry out God's will on Earth.

At AS and A Level you will need to show understanding and evaluation of the different ways in which Jesus has authority: as a moral teacher of wisdom, as Son of God, and as liberator of the oppressed.

You need to show understanding and **EXEGESIS** of the following Biblical passages:

• Mark 6:47-52   **WALKING ON WATER**

• John 9:1-41   **HEALING OF THE MAN BORN BLIND**

• Matthew 5:17-48 **FULFILMENT OF THE LAW** - revised the **TORAH**

• Luke 15:11-32   **PARABLE OF LOST SON (WAITING FATHER)**

• Mark 5:24-34   **AN UNCLEAN (BLEEDING) WOMAN**

• Luke 10:25-37   **PARABLE OF GOOD SAMARITAN**

Key Terms

- **FORM OF LIFE** - the historical, sociological, moral, and cultural conditions within which language operates. Associated with Wittgenstein.

- **TORAH** - first five books of the Hebrew Bible (Genesis, Exodus, Leviticus, Deuteronomy and Numbers).

- **SERMON ON THE MOUNT** - Matthew 5-7. Jesus' longest address of ethics.

- **METANOIA** - repentance, a radical change of heart.

- **PARABLE OF THE LOST SON** - Luke 15:11-32; deals with theme of lost and found.

- **ZEALOTS** - 1st Century Jewish political group. Sought to overcome Roman occupation in the rebellion of 66 AD and committed mass suicide at **MASADA** (AD 74)

- **UNDERSIDE OF HISTORY** - occupies a significant proportion of human existence but often forgotten. Sometimes refers to the oppressed or marginalised.

- **PREFERENTIAL OPTION FOR THE POOR** - Christian duty to side with the marginalised and to act against injustice.

- **SAMARITANS** - from Samaria. Regarded as racially and religiously impure as they had married foreigners and built their own temple.

- **SON OF GOD** - used by followers of Jesus describing Jesus' special relationship with God.

- **COUNCIL OF CHALCEDON -** 451 AD – re-affirm central Christian beliefs, particularly divinity and humanity of Jesus.

- **CHRISTOLOGY -** concerned with nature of Jesus' relationship with God.

- **INCARNATION -** 'in the flesh'.

- **THEOTOKOS -** 'God-bearer'.

- **DOCETIC -** Jesus only 'appeared' to be fully human so that God could communicate with humans.

- **EXEGESIS -** close analysis and interpretation of a text.

- **CHRIST-EVENT -** Jesus' birth, ministry, death, and resurrection.

Structure of Thought

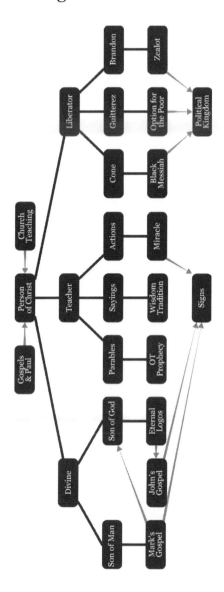

Jesus of History and the Christ of Faith

1. E.P. Sanders

- **FAITH** claims are different to claims made in the realm of reason.

- **HISTORICAL JESUS** shows a man acting within the laws of science and the limits of history. It would be a **CATEGORY MISTAKE** to venture into **HISTORY** as we would confuse history with faith.

- Jesus' teachings on hope for outcasts, non-violence and God's grace did make him significantly different to people at the time but not unique. Groups like the **ESSENES** established desert communities and taught of a coming kingdom.

2. Rudolph Bultmann

- The Jesus of history is less important than the **CHRIST OF FAITH.**

- The most we can know is the preaching/ teaching following Jesus' death (**KERYGMA** - the gospel of the early church).

- We should Evil and suffering can lead to belief without trust. **DEMYTHOLOGISE** the Bible (eg supposed events such as resurrection and ascension have spiritual meaning, not literal).

- The basis of Christian faith is the reflections of the early Church, inspired by their ongoing experiences of Christ; rather than the historical Jesus – of whom we can know **"almost nothing"**.

3. Black Messiah - James Cone

- Starting point is **HISTORICAL** – suffering and oppression of black people

- Link to **PAUL TILLICH** – theology reflects the culture of its day and emerges from it

- Jesus is given many **TITLES** in the NT – 'Son of David', 'Good Shepherd', 'Son of God'. 'Black Messiah' continues this tradition. Jesus would not have been white. Metaphor - Jesus' suffering in unity with the oppressed.

- **CROSS** – not just a symbol, it resonates with the **'lynching tree'**. Both Jesus and blacks died and suffered – on a cross – as a result of injustice.

Jesus Christ's Authority as Son of God

Expressed In his Knowledge of God, Miracles and Resurrection

1. Son of God and Messiah (Mark 6:47-52; John 9:1-41)

In Jewish terms, often used to refer to the King, anointed by God to do His will on Earth. Hoped that an anointed person would deliver Israel politically, morally and spiritually.

- Hebrew for anointed – **MESSIAH**

- Greek for anointed – **CHRISTOS**

- Son of God = **CHRIST**(os)

"Truly this man was God's Son!" (Mark 15:39) – remarked by Roman Centurion at Jesus' death. It is unclear whether the centurion meant Jesus was

the Son of God or **a** son of God.

Christian leaders accepted Jesus as both fully God and fully human.

2. Christology from Above

- Focus is on Jesus' **DIVINITY** and God's act of bringing humanity back into relationship with him.

- Known as **HIGH CHRISTOLOGY**.

- Relies on faith, cannot be proved.

3. Christology from Below

- Focus is on Jesus' **MESSAGE**, teaching and the example he sets.

- The focus of salvation is on how people **RESPOND** to Jesus and the way this helps to develop their relationship to God and the world.

- Known as **LOW CHRISTOLOGY**.

4. Did Jesus Think He Was Son of God?

- If Jesus thought he was fully human – how can we claim he knew he was God's Son?

- In **EXODUS**, God reveals his identity as "I am who I am"(Exodus 3:14).

- **JOHN**'s Gospel - Jesus uses similar statements - "I am the way, and the truth, and the life. No one comes to the Father except through me" (John 14:6).

- "The Father is **GREATER** than I" (John14:28). Does this imply that Jesus saw himself as limited by his own humanity?

- In **MARK 16:42** Jesus is asked "Are you the **CHRIST**, Son of the Blessed One?". When Jesus replies **I AM** the High Priest tears his clothes with rage and asks "do we need witnesses?" because he recognises the **BLASPHEMY** of invoking **YAHWEH**'s name (I Am who I Am).

5. Miracles do not necessarily indicate Jesus' Divinity

- Miracles - special insights into Jesus' teaching on the nature of God's **KINGDOM**. Example - Rich Man and Lazarus, last are **FIRST** (Luke 16)

- No single word for 'miracle' in New Testament. They might not point to the laws of nature being broken. Instead, 'mighty works', '**SIGNS**' and 'wonders' indicate something deeper about the nature of God and reality.

- **LOW CHRISTOLOGY** – Jesus' miracles understood like parables of **CREATION** (such as stilling the storm) or **REDEMPTION** (such as raising the paralysed man with the words 'your sins are forgiven", Mark 2) raises the issue - is he the **CREATOR-REDEEMER** incarnate?

6. Birth and Incarnation

- **Luke 1:35** – Jesus born of a Virgin, Mary.

- **Chalcedonian Definition** – Mary conceives God in human form – incarnation.

- Mary – **THEOTOKOS** (God-bearer).The Council of Ephesus decreed in 431 that Mary is the Theotokos because her son Jesus is both God and man: one divine person with two natures (divine and human) intimately and

HYPOSTATICALLY united (humanity and divinity in one hypostasis, or individual existence).

Some Heretical Views

NESTORIUS (d.c.451) – Christ's divine and human natures were completely separate. Humanity and divinity come together as one when Jesus' will becomes one with God's will.

APOLLINARIUS (c.310-390) – Incarnation meant that God's will replaced Jesus' human reason. Jesus was a complete person and experienced suffering, still had a soul but could not sin as he would have no 'inner conflict'.

DOCETIC CHRISTIANS – Incarnation involved God only appearing to assume human flesh. Jesus could not have been fully human as he was fully God, bringing salvation through this knowledge.

Miracles as Signs of Salvation

1. Redemption and Creation Miracles

Agreed by both **HIGH** and **LOW** Christologies.

Echoes vision of **ISAIAH** of a renewed society with new insight.

• E.g. **healing of man born blind** (John 9:1-41) focuses more on the man's awareness of Jesus as saviour, than on the process of the man's sight being saved. **REDEMPTION MIRACLE**.

• **Jesus' walking on water** (Mark 6:47-52) indicates how salvation applies to the whole of the universe; reminiscent of God's spirit hovering over the chaotic water at the point of Creation (Genesis 1:2). **CREATION MIRACLE.**

2. Resurrection as Miracle

A Jewish idea taught by **PHARISEES** that the righteous would be raised to live in God's Kingdom at the end of time.

Jesus' resurrection was different – witnessed by many over a long period; marked the beginning of a **NEW ERA** as early followers experienced a change in their relationship with God.

St PAUL – everything can be brought into completion by God. The resurrection was the '**FIRST FRUITS**' (1 Corinthians 15:20)

WOLFHART PANNENBURG – Jesus was an ordinary human in his lifetime but the resurrection was a decisive moment in history, a unique sign of God's accomplishment of creation at the end of days, revealing Jesus as God's Son.

3. Doubting Thomas

"Then he said to Thomas, 'Put your finger here and see my hands. Reach out your hand and put it in my side. Do not doubt but believe.' Thomas answered him, 'My Lord and my God!'". (John 20:27-28).

Jesus' body is not just transformed spiritually but also allows the experience of the presence of God. A **RELIGIOUS EXPERIENCE** – Jesus' resurrection allows him to be witnessed to and worshipped as God without being blasphemous. Those who believe '**WITHOUT SEEING**' are commended. (John 20). The resurrection gives authority to proclaim Jesus as God's Son.

Jesus as Moral Teacher

Jesus' moral teaching on repentance and forgiveness, inner purity and moral motivation (Matthew 5:17-48; Luke 15:11-32)

1. The Living Word (John 1)

WITTGENSTEIN - Jesus' authority is derived from him as a teacher of wisdom. He affirmed **AUTHENTIC LIVING.**

Jesus embodied the **MORAL** and **SPIRITUAL** and so was the **LIVING WORD** ('The word became flesh and lived among us', John 1)

2. Jesus' Moral Teaching

Jesus uses **PARABLES**, short sayings, actions, examples and healings to express moral message.

Jesus as the **NEW MOSES** founding a **NEW ISRAEL** (argument of theologian **TOM WRIGHT**). A new community of the KIngdom of God.

"Do not think that I have come to abolish the Law or the Prophets; I have not come to abolish them but to **FULFIL** them." (Matthew 5:17).

3. Forgiveness and Repentance

METANOIA (repentance or radical change of heart) – At the heart of Jesus' teaching on the arrival of the Kingdom of God.

Examples include **ZACCHAEUS** (tax collector) and the **PARABLE OF THE PRODIGAL SON** (Luke 15: 11-32)

Forgiveness brings about mental (end of guilt) and material freedom (forgive our debts) and restores/heals relationships.

Seen in Lord's Prayer.

4. Personal Responsibility

Keeping the Sabbath holy is an important religious law **(Ten Commandments, Exodus 20:1-17).**

It is also an important social law as it is a **foundation for social justice** – everyone is entitled to one day free from work during the week.

Jesus argued people misused Sabbath rules in order to avoid social responsibility. Rabbis had developed 39 different definitions and examples of work (which had to be avoided). Jesus argued that **in focusing on this religious duty, people were avoiding their duty to humanity.**

"The Sabbath was made for humankind, not humankind for the Sabbath" (Jesus, Mark 2:27).

Despite the risk of death penalty for breaking the Sabbath rules, Jesus broke these to heal the sick and allowed his disciples to 'pick corn' to eat.

Morality is not 'blind obedience'. It requires personal responsibility and **PURITY** of mind.

Religious practices should serve human **NEEDS**.

Jesus as Liberator

Jesus' role as liberator of the marginalised, his challenge to political & religious authority (Mark 5:24-34; Luke 10:25-37).

Some Key Authors

1. S.G.F.BRANDON JESUS AND THE ZEALOTS (1967) - later writers made Jesus out to be a pacifist, toning down the reality that he was in fact a politically-driven activist – a freedom fighter.

• Preferential Option for the Poor

• The Underside of History

Jesus shows a bias to these groups, despite the Church presenting him as politically neutral, a spiritual teacher.

2. GUSTAVO GUTIÉRREZ (1928-) **A THEOLOGY OF LIBERATION**

• Father of **LIBERATION THEOLOGY**

• Seeing Jesus as liberator makes him (the Christ of faith) 'really engaged' in the world and allows us to see the people of the Bible as more than just fictitious characters

• Jesus' historical example as **PREFERENTIAL OPTION FOR THE POOR** sets the expectation for modern Christians

• Jesus more than a **ZEALOT** - did not set himself up as a national leader - encouraged his followers not to think of him in that way. Jesus' mission was also not only to save Israel but **ALL** human societies.

3. CAMILLO TORRES RESTREPO (1929-66) ROMAN CATHOLIC PRIEST

- Joined communist guerrilla group (National Libertarian Army of Columbia) in their active resistance against the government.

- No longer a priest by the time of fighting but still thought of his actions in a priestly way.

Liberator of the Marginalised

Many parables deal with help of the outcast – often, sinners (**HAMARTALOI**). These include the 'unclean' (diseased, paralysed), tax collectors, sexually impure, religious heretics and the uneducated (fishermen, labourers), as in **LEVITICAL CODE** of OT law.

Jesus - **MORAL MESSAGE** - often delivered through his example towards those considered impure, rather than the religious leaders.

- Luke 10:25-37 (Good Samaritan)

- Mark 5:24-34 (contrast with Leviticus 15:19-28) Bleeding Woman

- "The last shall be first, and the first last" (Matthew 20:16).

Jesus ejected table-fellowship **RITUALS** of the Pharisees (ritual washing, food laws etc.) Indicates his vision of the Kingdom of God as a transformed society. In **MARK 7** he declares all foods "clean'.

Possible Exam Questions

1. "There is no evidence to suggest that Jesus thought of himself as divine." Discuss.

2. To what extent can Jesus be regarded as no more than a teacher of wisdom?

3. "Jesus' role was just to liberate the poor and weak against oppression." Discuss.

4. Assess the view that the miracles prove Jesus was the Son of God.

5. "Jesus Christ is not unique." Discuss.

6. To what extent was Jesus just a teacher of morality?

Key Quotes

"The use of such words as 'unique' and 'unprecedented' shows that [scholars] have shifted their perspective from that of critical history and exegesis to that of faith." (E.P. Sanders, Jesus and Judaism, p. 320).

"Christ's blackness is both literal and symbolic. His blackness is literal in the sense that he truly becomes One with the oppressed blacks, taking their suffering as his suffering and revealing that he is found in the history of our struggle, the story of our pain." (J. Cone, God of the Oppressed, p. 136).

"The Father and I are one" (John 10:30).

"Whoever has seen me has seen the Father" (John 14:9).

"Jesus accompanies his words with many 'mighty works and wonders and signs' which manifest that the kingdom is present in him and attest that he was the promised Messiah." (Catechism of the Catholic Church para. 547).

"So miracles strengthen faith in the One who does his Father's works; they bear witness that he is the Son of God" (Catechism of the Catholic Church para. 548).

"Only because the end of the world is already present in Jesus' resurrection is God revealed in him" (W. Pannenberg, Jesus – God and Man, 1968, p. 69).

"Jesus said, "My kingdom is not of this world. If it were, my servants would fight to prevent my arrest by the Jewish leaders. But now my kingdom is from another place." (John 18:36).

"The duty of every Catholic is to be a revolutionary. The duty of every revolutionary is to make the revolution" (Restrepo, speech, 1965, cited in Wilcockson, Wilkinson, & Campbell, 2016, p. 311).

"If Jesus were alive today, He would be a guerrillero" (Restrepo, cited in Wilcockson, Wilkinson, & Campbell, 2016, p. 311).

Christian Moral Principles

Diversity of Christian Moral Reasoning, Practices & Sources of Ethics

Background and Influences

"All Scripture is inspired by God, and is useful for teaching, for reproof, for correction, for training in righteousness" (2 Timothy 3:16).

The following questions are relevant:

1. If the Bible does reveal God's will and if it is true that only Biblical ethical commands must be followed; then what can be helpful in discerning how to follow scripture?

2. If God is the author of the Bible, does this mean that it, alone, must be used for moral instruction?

3. If the Bible is **INFALLIBLE,** and we cannot understand it, is the problem with the reader rather than with the text?

At A Level, you will need to show understanding and evaluation of the Bible as the only authority for Christian ethical practices; Bible, Church and reason as the sources of Christian ethical practices; and love (**AGAPE**) as the only Christian ethical principle which governs Christian practices.

Key Terms

- **AGAPE** - Greek for 'love'. Also, refers to Jesus' sacrificial and generous love for others

- **AUTONOMOUS CHRISTIAN ETHICS** - ethics are self-governed.

- **BIBLICISM** - belief that the Bible is the revealed word of God and that God directly inspired the writers of the Bible.

- **COVENANT** - God's special promises and agreement made with humans which requires special behaviour from them.

- **HETERONOMOUS CHRISTIAN ETHICS** - several sources of authority or law govern ethics (eg Natural Law, Bible, Reason).

- **HERMENEUTICAL** - study of the principles of interpreting the Bible

- **MAGISTERIUM** - the official teaching of the Church entrusted to the Pope and his bishops (eg in the **CATECHISM** and **ENCYCLICALS**)

- **PAPAL ENCYCLICAL** - letter issued by the Pope to his senior clergy on some significant topic or teaching; has doctrinal authority.

- **PRIMA SCRIPTURA** - the Bible is the principle source of authority but is understood through and with Church teaching and reason.

- **SOLA SCRIPTURA** - exclusive following of the Bible.

- **THEONOMOUS CHRISTIAN ETHICS** - God's law or commands govern ethics. Living the good life must be revealed by God, since we are by nature, sinful.

Structure of Thought

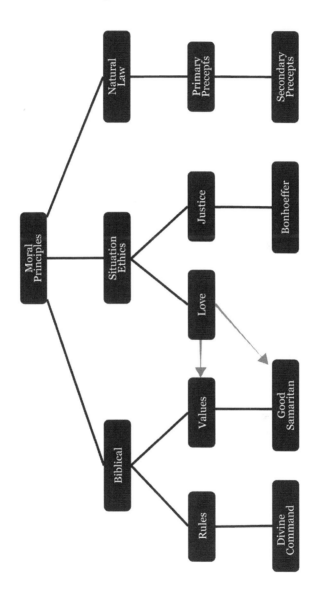

Different Approaches to a Christian Moral Reading of the Bible

Hermeneutic (Interpretation) Factors

Richard B. HAYS proposes many factors to consider when thinking about how Christians use the Bible to help them to make moral decisions.

1. **Accuracy** different gospels relate slightly different versions

2. **Range** of issues may be limited by cultural context

3. **Frequency** of use of sections

4. **Management** of different texts

5. **Focal images** metaphors can be interpreted different ways

MNEMONIC: Angus Ran For Max's Football

HAYS also proposed questions of interpretation (**HERMENEUTICS**):

1. Is there a focus on **symbolism**?

2. Is there a focus on **rules**?

3. Is there a focus on **principles**?

4. Is there a focus on **paradigms**?

MNEMONIC: Sophie Really Painted Poppies

Propositional & Non-Propositional Revelation

- **PROPOSITIONAL KNOWLEDGE** - knowing or accepting something as true e.g. knowing the date of your birthday. Has a truth value – can be true, false, or somewhere in the middle.

- **PROPOSITIONAL REVELATION** - knowledge revealed by God, not through reason e.g. God's moral standards (such as the Ten Commandments).

- **PROPOSITIONAL APPROACH TO THE BIBLE** - the words in the Bible are messages from God. There are fixed moral messages and meanings e.g. in parables and Sermon on the Mount.

- **NON-PROPOSITIONAL KNOWLEDGE** - other kinds of knowledge e.g. how to do something.

- **NON-PROPOSITIONAL REVELATION** - belief or faith in God through personal encounter or experience.

- **NON-PROPOSITIONAL APPROACH TO THE BIBLE** - God's revelation in Jesus was through Jesus' human life, not through a book. The Bible acts as a doorway into meeting the living God.

The Bible as Sole Authority for Ethics

If the Bible reveals God's will, then only Bible commands must be followed

1. Ethics can be shown in the Bible as **THEONOMOUS**.

2. Ethics can be expressed through **COVENANT** (a legal agreement).

THEONOMOUS ethics are shown through real life situations, rather than as clear commandments.

E.g. King **DAVID**'s adultery with Bathsheba (2 Samuel 11) illustrates what living 'the moral life' is NOT. David is not just judged on his adherence to the commandments but on the type of person he became. Uriah (Bathsheba's husband who was killed in battle) strikes a complete contrast.

Must be understood in the theological context of life lived as a **COVENANT** agreement with mutual obligations, with God.

The **OLD TESTAMENT** establishes ethics as both **SOCIAL** and **PERSONAL**. The **TEN COMMANDMENTS** are evidence of this (Exodus 20:1-17). Other Biblical examples:

- **AMOS** and **ISAIAH** – Old Testament Prophets – focus on social justice and see a proper response to God's covenant to be treatment of the **POOR.**

- New Testament: Jesus' **SERMON** on the **MOUNT**(Matthew 5-7) – the new covenant is not just about following the laws set out in the Old Testament but involves the inner laws of love, peace, faith, and righteousness – "be perfect as your heavenly Father is perfect" (Matthew 5:48).

- Modelled on Jesus' sacrifice, St **PAUL** uses '**LIVING SACRIFICE**' (Romans 12:1) to describe Christian covenantal life. This makes devotion to God and love of neighbour above anything else.

Literalism - Is It Realistic?

"If your right eye causes you to sin, tear it out and throw it away" (Matthew 5:29).

KARL BARTH argued that scripture has high value, but literalism could be dangerous as it gives the bible a divine status that can only rightly be given to God. This is **BIBLIOLATRY** – false worship of the Bible.

Words of the bible are a **WITNESS** to God's Word revealed through the different writers of the Bible over time. It is not the 'Word' itself. Bible writers were 'inspired' but God did not dictate the Bible.

Bible must be read **CRITICALLY** as a source of inspiration. It is not truth itself, despite being a source of moral truth.

HUMAN REASON must be taken into account.

Contradictions

1. Old Testament

There is a contradiction between war and **RETRIBUTIVE JUSTICE**: "an eye for an eye, a tooth for a tooth" (Exodus 21:24) and Jesus' pronouncement to 'love your enemy' (Matthew 5:44) and 'turn teh other cheek'.

The sanctity of human life is contradicted by capital punishment apparent for **BLASPHEMY** (Genesis 9:6).

Capital punishment for those who undermine social and divine order, adultery (Deuteronomy 22:22); dishonouring **PARENTS** (Numbers 1:51), **HOMOSEXUAL** acts (Leviticus 18).

Deuteronomy 20:10-20 – sets out rules of **WAR**, Israelites allowed to kill foreign women and children of the coastal tribes. Again this contradicts the idea of the sanctity of human life, **THOU SHALT NOT KILL.** (Exodus 20:13)

2. New Testament

Sermon on the Mount (Matthew 5-7) – consciously revises old law of **LEVITICUS** (eg 'eye for an eye' becomes 'turn the other cheek') - the **PURITY**

CODE is demolished by Jesus eg touching 'unclean women'.

RECONCILIATION replaces retribution (**Matthew 5:38-42**) and love of enemies is taught in addition (**Matthew 5:44**).

Jesus stressing a future ideal – **KINGDOM OF GOD**, similar to how previous prophets in the Old testament had ventured (**Micah 4:1-4**).

Meanwhile, in an imperfect world, violence might be a **NECESSARY EVIL** (Augustine, Luther).

Others argue Biblical **PACIFISM** (Martin **LUTHER KING** Jr) is a Christian duty as it lay at heart of Jesus' teaching on love.

Strengths of Bible - Sole Authority

1. Makes the Bible **INFALLIBLE** (unchallengeable) and **INERRANT** (no mistakes).

2. Can be trusted and relied upon **AS INSPIRED BY GOD** (2 Timothy 3:16).

3. **RICHARD MOUW** – "just because there is one biblical commandment, a law of love, does not rule out the possibility of other biblical commandments on other matters" (Summarised and cited in Ahluwalia & Bowie, 2016, p. 392).

4. Seeing the Bible as infallible can provide a helpful framework for living – decisions about **TAKING LIFE** (Sermon on Mount); attitudes towards **SEXUALITY** (Old Testament, St Paul); attitudes towards **MARRIAGE** (Genesis and Jesus' teachings).

Weaknesses of Bible as Sole Authority

1. We can't separate ourselves from our own reading of the text – impossible not to read **subjectively** and with **interpretation**.

2. If God dictated, then why so many **different styles** e.g. John's Gospel is much more mystical and theological.

3. **Conflicts** arise – Jesus' attitude to Jewish laws eg Leviticus and the bleeding woman of Mark 5 (no longer unclean, as Jesus accepts her).

4. Many Christians do not follow all the 'rules' in the Bible and some do not even appear to refer to moral living e.g. **LEVITICUS 19:27** limits the cutting of facial and head hair; Leviticus 19:19 bans planting two crops in the same field.

Bible Church & Reason

Christian Ethics must involve a combination of Biblical teaching, Church teaching and human reason.

Christian ethics should combine Biblical and Church teaching with human **REASON** to account for new situations.

- **PRIMA SCRIPTURA** – the Bible is the principle source of authority but is understood through and with Church teaching and reason.

- **RICHARD HAYS** and **WILLIAM SPOHN** – you cannot study scripture without reference to the Church communities and traditions. **SPOHN** suggests three interconnecting pillars: 1. the New Testament story of Jesus; 2. the ethics of virtue and character; and 3. the practices of Christian spirituality.

Ethical Heteronomy - Roman Catholicism

Christian ethics can be accessed through the **NATURAL WORLD, CHURCH AUTHORITY, REASON** and **THE BIBLE**. Together, these make up the **NATURAL LAW**.

Biblical grounding – Romans 2:15 – even **GENTILES** (non-Jews) can behave morally when acting according to their conscience and 'the law of God written on their hearts'.

Thomas Aquinas' Natural Law

Humans are set apart from other animals because of our ability to use human reason to know God's **ETERNAL LAW**.

Human experience of God's eternal law is based on **SELF-EVIDENT** principle – do good, avoid evil - **SYNDERESIS**. Goodness is the **GOAL** of human flourishing.

Magisterium - Roman Catholic

COLLECTIVE WISDOM of Church leaders and teachers, published in **PAPAL ENCYCLICALS** (circulated letters).

In all ordinary circumstances, the **MAGISTERIUM** should be followed – it has authority.

"The Church, the 'pillar and bulwark of the truth', 'has received this solemn command of Christ from the apostles to announce the saving truth'." (Catechism of the Catholic Church, 2032).

Veritatis Splendor (Splendour of Truth)

1996, Pope John Paul II – **VERITATIS SPLENDOR** – **ENCYCLICAL** reasserts centrality of reason, conscience, natural law, and Magisterium in Catholic moral theology.

Moral law = knowable to all through **REASON, NATURAL LAW** and **CONSCIENCE**.

Humans are **SINFUL** and cannot rely on reason alone. Church acts as a guide.

Some moral acts are **INTRINSICALLY** wrong (wrong in **THEMSELVES)**. It is never right to contradict the moral order.

Liberation Theology

Developed from1960s onwards - popular in **LATIN AMERICA**.

Bible is seen as the centre of ethics, particularly the **EXODUS** story and other stories of liberation from **SLAVERY**.

ETHICS FROM BELOW– begins with the marginalised, **ENGAGES** with political and economic struggles against the **POWERS**; suspicious of 'top-down' traditional Church teaching.

Some use of **MARXISM**, but criticised, as while it is good at questioning power, it also criticises religion for being exploitative and an **OPIUM OF THE PEOPLE** reinforcing false consciousness (acceptance) of their oppression.

Conscience & Tradition

Protestant **NATURAL LAW** theologians – Richard **HOOKER** (1554-1600); Hugo **GROTIUS** (1583-1645). Bible evolved over time, developing out of the needs of communities and therefore reason and conscience should guide its use in ethics (like Catholicism but no magisterium).

Stanley Hauerwas

Christian ethics can only be done in the Christian worshipping community, called **BASE COMMUNITIES.**

Jesus adapted Old Testament teaching in his **Sermon on the Mount** and we continue to **adapt tradition** today.

Jesus' sermon was aimed at Christian community, not leaders. It includes examples of Christian values that must be developed in communities, in response to God, siding with the **MARGINALISED**.

Christian communities need to question society's values by living and practising Christian **SOCIAL VIRTUES** (loyalty, trust, faithfulness, forgiveness, reconciliation).

Criticisms of the Bible, Faith & Reason

1. Problem of **Sources**: What are legitimate sources for Christian ethics? Are some sources e.g. Marxism, alien to Christian thinking? Do some sources have greater authority than others? If so, what principles determine the hierarchy of these sources?

2. Deviation from Bible: some accuse Catholic tradition of breaking away from the Bible e.g. Martin **LUTHER**, German Reformer.

3. Jesus' attitude to **Tradition:** Jesus appears to criticise religious traditions e.g. Pharisees' focus on ritual cleanliness.

4. Law of love: should prevail over traditions (Rudolf **BULTMANN**).

5. Justice, love, and wisdom: three ethical norms that should work together for Christians (Paul **TILLICH**), the most important of which is love and not the following of fixed rules that influence '**MORAL PURITANISM**' – the groups that aligns the Christian message with fixed rules about foods, drinks, and sexual relations.

MNEMONIC: Scrt David's Traditional Lovely Pie

Agape Love is All

Jesus' only command was to love and human reason must decide how to apply this (Fletcher's Situation Ethics)

Autonomous

LOVE should be the only governing Christian principle – summarised in Jesus' own sacrificial life

Hans Küng: supports **AUTONOMY**.

There is nothing in Christian ethics that could not be found in any person with good will.

Pope **FRANCIS** encourages moral guidance rooted in love. The rules of Catholic tradition should be recognised but so should modern challenges of human relationships.

Applied to Euthanasia

Contrary to official Catholic moral teaching but not the principles of Catholic reasoning and conscience to keep someone alive at all costs.

Jesus specifically challenged rule-based ethics and encouraged autonomy. (Mark 7:14-23) - Jesus declares all foods **CLEAN** in opposition to Levitical purity code..

We should not ask if euthanasia is right or wrong but rather, does it respect a person's life?

Rejected by 'faith-ethic' Catholic theologians for undermining Magisterium - official Catholic Church teaching e.g. Joseph **RATZINGER** (Pope Benedict XVI).

Possible Exam Questions

1. How fair is the claim that there is nothing distinctive about Christian ethics?

2. "The Bible is all that is needed as a moral guide for Christian behaviour." Discuss.

3. "The Church should decide what is morally good." Discuss.

4. Assess the view that the Bible is a comprehensive moral guide for Christians.

5. To what extent do Christians actually disagree about what Christian ethics are?

6. "Christian moral principles are not self-evident." Discuss.

Key Quotes

"Prophecy never had its origin in the human will, but prophets, though human, spoke from God as they were carried along by the Holy Spirit". 2 Peter 1:20-21.

"Then the Lord reached out his hand and touched my mouth and said to me, 'I have put my words in your mouth.'" Jeremiah 1:9.

"Just because there is one biblical commandment, a law of love, does not rule out the possibility of other biblical commandments on other matters" (Richad Mouw, surmised and cited in Ahluwalia & Bowie, 2016, p. 392). "

The interpretation of Scripture can never occur in a vacuum". (Richard Hays, The Moral Vision of the New Testament, 1996, p. 209).

"Sacred tradition and Sacred Scripture form one sacred deposit of the word of God, committed to the Church". (Vatican II Council, Dei Verbum, 'Dogmatic Constitution on Divine Revelation,' par. 10. In Vatican Council II: The Conciliar Documents, ed. Flannery, 1975.

"This teaching office [magisterium] is not above the Word of God, but serves it". (Vatican II Council, Dei Verbum, 'Dogmatic Constitution on Divine Revelation,' par. 10. In Vatican Council II: The Conciliar Documents, ed. Flannery, 1975.

"The Church, the 'pillar and bulwark of the truth', 'has received this solemn command of Christ from the apostles to announce the saving truth'." Catechism of the Catholic Church para. 2032.

"This is my commandment, that you love one another as I have loved you. No one has greater love than this, to lay down one's life for one's friends" (John 15:12-13).

"Love does not delight in evil but rejoices with the truth. 7 It always protects, always trusts, always hopes, always perseveres." St Paul (1 Cor. 13:6-7).

1 "All Scripture is inspired by God and profitable for teaching, for rebuke and for training in righteousness". (1 Timothy, 3:16)

Christian Moral Action

Background & Influences

- **BONHOEFFER'S ETHICS** - Our sinful nature means that no human decision can with certainty be declared absolutely right or wrong. Sometimes, we can act only **out of despair but in faith and hope.** It is impossible to accurately predict all possible outcomes of an action. Consequentialist approaches to moral action are rejected.

- **MARTIN LUTHER** - State rule brought order to the natural sinful inclination of humans towards disorder. Bonhoeffer was different and emphasised the **AUTHORITY** of God over that of the state. Luther supported the suppression of the **PEASANT**'s revolt in Germany (1534-6).

"They have doubly deserved death in body and soul as murderers... they cloak this horrible sin with the gospel." (Luther,,1535)

At A Level, you must evaluate the teaching and example of Bonhoeffer on **DUTY** to God and **DUTY** to the State, the Church as community and source of spiritual discipline, and the **COST** of discipleship.

Key Terms

- **CHEAP GRACE** - grace that is offered freely, but is received without any change in the person.

- **CONSEQUENTIAL ETHICS** - any form of ethics which judges the rightness or wrongness of an act by its outcomes.

- **COSTLY GRACE** - grace followed by obedience to God's command and discipleship.

- **DISCIPLESHIP** - following the life, teaching, and example of Jesus.

- **LIBERAL SOCIETIES** - societies which develop their laws based on the principle that humans flourish when given maximum freedoms and minimum control by governments.

- **NO RUSTY SWORDS** - Bonhoeffer's metaphor to describe the outworn ethical attitudes which the Church has used and have no use for today.

- **PASSION** - Jesus' sufferings at the end of his life.

- **RELIGIONLESS CHRISTIANITY** - Bonhoeffer's description of Christianity without the baggage of the past and contamination by the ideological beliefs of the present.

- **SECULAR PACIFISM** - secular means 'of this world'. Pacifism - violence and war are wrong. Bonhoeffer invented the term 'secular pacifism' to show a false non-religious belief that society can achieve a state of non-violence.

- **SOLIDARITY** - an selfless commitment to stand alongside, and be with those less fortunate.

- **THE WESTERN VOID** - Bonhoeffer's description of the state of the Western secular world without Christianity filled with all kinds of dangerous beliefs and ideas.

- **WORLD COME OF AGE** - used by Bonhoeffer to describe how the Western culture has grown up and in embracing a rational view of the world has discarded a superstitious view of religion.

Structure of Thought

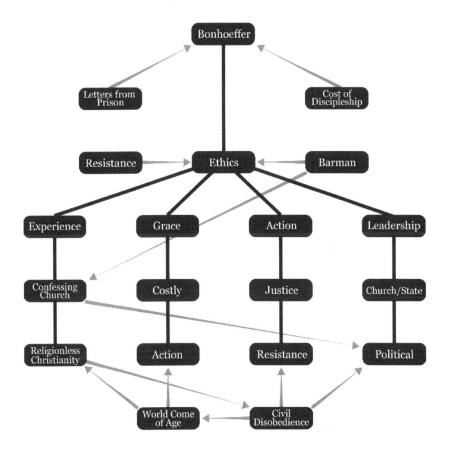

Duty to God & the State

Responsibility to the State

Bonhoeffer taught Christians have a **RESPONSIBILITY** to the state. They must work to ensure the state acts according to **GOD'S WILL**.

Sometimes, the state gains too much power and **JUSTICE** is set below policy. Other times, the state assumes it is 'justice itself' and uses this to justify any action. The state fails to acknowledge its **OBEDIENCE TO THE WILL OF GOD**.

BONHOEFFER – the state can **NEVER** represent the will of God and therefore, the state can **NEVER** adopt ultimate power.

The Church is to keep the state in check – not be a part of it.

Obedience, Leadership & Doing God's Will

Christians have a duty to **DISOBEY** if the state is making reasonable people face difficult situations.

The Church was being fooled into believing **NAZISM** was bringing order to a disordered society.

"Hitler is the way of the Spirit and the will of God for the German people to enter the church of Christ" (Hermann Gruner, quoted in Geffrey B. Kelly et al., Dietrich Bonhoeffer: The Life of a Modern Martyr (Christianity Today Essentials, 2012)

The ostracism of minorities and disrespect for life was a disregard for **GOD-GIVEN ORDER**.

Establishing social order may justify **TYRANNICIDE** as a Christian duty.

A Christian can only act in faith and in hope – influenced by **MARTIN LUTHER** - **'here I stand, I can do no other'**.

LUTHERAN TEACHING – God ordained two kingdoms:

1. The **SPIRITUAL** kingdom of Christ, governed by the Church

2. The **POLITICAL** kingdom of the world, governed by the state

We should ask if obeying the state is the will of God. This will only be clear in the **INSTANT OF ACTION** and as an act of faith.

"You can only know what obedience is by obeying. It is no use asking questions; for it is only through obedience that you come to learn the truth" (Dietrich Bonhoeffer, The Cost of discipleship, 1959, p. 68)

"There is no road to faith or discipleship, no other road – only obedience to the call of Jesus" (Dietrich Bonhoeffer, The Cost of discipleship, 1959, p. 49)

Justification for Civil Disobedience

It is impossible to know whether our actions are truly good or not. No amount of human reason can morally justify killing.

BONHOEFFER argues to kill Hitler and disobey the state is only justified by **'bold action as the free response to faith'**. It cannot be justified in ordinary **ETHICAL TERMS**.

Love is not the only **MORAL PRINCIPLE** by which we can live the moral life. Human ideas **ENSLAVE** humans. Humans are only freed by responding to **GOD'S WILL**.

Consolation for civil disobedience, such as the assassination attempt on Hitler is possible only through God's promises to forgive the '**man who becomes a sinner in the process**' (Letters and Papers from Prison, p. 138).

Duty to God outweighs duty to the State. Need to break away from Luther's idea of advocating of obedience to civil authority.

You would be just as guilty for the destruction of a town if you did nothing, as you would be if you were among those who helped to burn it down. If you are acting out of love, as Christian ethics demands, you need to **actively challenge injustice and resist it** (Link **SYNOPTICALLY** to Fletcher's **SITUATION ETHICS.**

Civil Disobedience - Examples

Bonhoeffer spoke against Nazi ideas in his **UNIVERSITY** position, and then against Nazism at public **LECTURES**. He was banned.

- Criticised **CONFESSING CHURCH** when it wavered under pressure from Hitler to conform.

- Participated in **ILLEGAL SEMINARY** for training pastors.

- Openly spoke about his **PRAYERS** for the defeat of his own country.

Proclaimed Hitler as the **ANTI-CHRIST:**

"Therefore we must go on with our work and eliminate him whether he is successful or not" (Kenny et al., Dietrich Bonhoeffer: The Life of a Modern Martyr [Christianity Today Essentials], 2012).

It is thought he joined the **STAUFFENBERG** plot to **ASSASSINATE** Hitler in

1944 (see the film **VALKYRIE -** the name of the plot**)**.

As a member of the German military intelligence, Bonhoeffer acted as a **DOUBLE AGENT** working with Resistance and Allies.

He was eventually caught when he helped to smuggle **JEWS** into Switzerland, posing as agents of military intelligence.

MNEMONIC: Uptown Lads Create Illuminated Acrobatics During Summer

Church - Community & Discipline

Like **KANT**, Bonhoeffer believed that a Christian can recognise that they act out of **DUTY** when they act along with the rest of humankind.

- The **MORAL AND SPIRITUAL COMMUNITY** of the Church provide the tools needed to live morally in this world. To do this, the Church needs to become **RELIGIONLESS**.

- The **WORLD COME OF AGE** was costly. In discarding Christian values as 'irrational', **LIBERALISM** brought about the **WESTERN VOID** - a **SPIRITUAL VACUUM** that Christianity used to occupy.

Bonhoeffer felt that **NATIONAL SOCIALISM** of the Nazis partly filled this void. Bonhoeffer called for a paradoxical **RELIGIONLESS CHRISTIANITY,** as he argued ethical attitudes used by the Church before have no use today and are 'outworn'- represented by Bonhoeffer's metaphors of **RUSTY SWORDS**. and of **SALT** and L**IGHT** – visible in the **SERMON ON THE MOUNT**. As salt adds flavour to food, Christians must be present among other people and must act as 'light' for the room in their moral actions.

The Confessing Church

When Christianity and National Socialism were blended, forming the German Christian movement, it triggered the founding of the **CONFESSING CHURCH.**

In **1934** Hitler amended the articles of the **GERMAN EVANGELICAL CHURCH** issuing the **ARYAN PARAGRAPH** which made it necessary for all clergy to be of Aryan descent. **BONHOEFFER** and Martin **NIEMOLLER** disagreed with this change and brought together others who also disagreed. This group formed the early **CONFESSING CHURCH**.

In **1934** the Confessing Church met in **BARMEN** and the foundations of **BARTH'S** 'Barmen Declaration' were formed. A Christian's primary **DUTY** is to **CHRIST** and Christians should reject any teaching that is not revealed in Jesus Christ.

The **BARMEN DECLARATION 1934** was a clear denial of Nazi **NATIONAL SOCIALISM** but some say its disobedience against the state was limited and it could have done more politically to aid Jews and other minority groups.

Bonhoeffer tried to take it further to be more **INCLUSIVE** and from this, came his **ECUMENICAL THEOLOGY** – a direct disagreement with the German Christian movement.

In line with '**RELIGIONLESS** Christianity', the confessing Church was not to become 'national' – there must be no racial, political, or national boundaries in a Christian community, as Jesus taught. Bonhoeffer argued "the Church is her true self when she exists for **HUMANITY**".

Finkenwalde

Following his return from the USA in **1935**, Bonhoeffer was responsible for constructing a community at **FINKENWALDE** for training clergy for the Confessing Church.

Nazi control of the German Church and the appointment of a **REICH BISHOP** led to a decline in suitable clergy. The **HIMMLER DECREE** of **1937** made the training of clergy for the Confessing Church illegal and Finkenwalde was shut down by the **THIRD REICH** in September.

The **VIRTUE OF DISCIPLINE** was thought to be the most practical of the Christian virtues and Finkenwalde was intended as a place to develop this through practical Christian living. Key features are listed below:

- *Discipline* - Life was basic and monastic. Both the body and the mind needed to be disciplined and well exercised. The group frequently went on long bike rides together.

- *Meditation* - Foundation of prayer, develops discipline.

- *Community for others* - No one is perfect and so the Church is not there for the righteous but for the forgiven. Needs to be 'outward looking' – Christ dies for all, not just for Christians.

- *Bible* - Heart of daily life for a Christian. An intelligent understanding of the development of Christian teaching was encouraged by debate and discussion.

- *Brotherhood* - Love of and for Christ binds together the community, sustained by the Holy Spirit. Former students Informed of developments and director should change often so that the group does not become 'stuck in its ways'.

The Cost of Discipleship

Bonhoeffer's teaching on Ethics as action

Christianity is grounded in the **EVERYDAY WORLD** – it is not an 'otherworldly institution'. This is affirmed in God's **INCARNATION** – where he took on human flesh, became man and lived among humankind. *"The word became flesh and dwelt among us"* (**JOHN 1**).

Rather than investigating God's nature as human/divine, we should be asking *'who is Christ for us today?'*

Bonhoeffer was influenced by Karl **BARTH**, a Swiss **CALVINIST** theologian. The meaning of Christianity is in action.

BARTH - we do not know God – it is God who chooses to **REVEAL** Himself to humans – always a special and never a general act. **BONHOEFFER** agrees but says we should be careful not to accept the limited role of 'passively receiving' revelation – *we must 'do' as well as 'hear' the law* - e.g. **PHARISEES** (a subdivision of Jewish religious teaches) listened to commands but did not act on God's behalf; and in Luke, Martha acts but fails to listen to Jesus' teaching. Jesus calls the Pharisees **"HYPOCRITES"**.

CONSCIENCE is the experience of disunity in the self – it prompts action. Ethics is action. Action is liberating.

Costly Grace

"When Christ calls a man, he bids him come and die...Suffering then, is the badge of true discipleship" (Bonhoeffer, The Cost of Discipleship, 1959, p. 79, p., 80)

Authentic Christianity must be based on:

• **CHRIST**

• **SCRIPTURE**

• **FAITH**

These are the three fundamentals. If we stray from these, then we only have human intervention and nothing else. Religion as an institution is a human invention - like politics.

Church must be **SEPARATE** from State if it is to avoid being politically manipulated.

In taking on the world, the Christian disciple endangers himself.

CHEAP GRACE e.g. rituals, cannot win God's grace. Rather, grace is 'costly'.

"Costly because it costs man his life, and it is grace because it gives man the only true life ... Above all, it is costly because it cost God the life of his Son" (The Cost of Discipleship, p. 5).

God's grace is '**FREELY GIVEN**' not earned. However, it should not be 'cheap' and taken for granted, under the cheap umbrella that Jesus died and saved us from our sins - we take the grace but avoid the cost. Churches are in danger of offering grace without the **COST** of discipleship, which for Jesus meant **SUFFERING** and "giving his life as a **RANSOM** for many" (**MARK 10.45**).

"Cheap grace is effectively a lie, it is not the grace of God but a self-congratulating grace we give ourselves" (Ahluwalia & Bowie, 2016, p. 421)

COSTLY GRACE for Bonhoeffer involved a realisation he might have to die, though he did not seek to suffer and never saw himself as a martyr. He wrote many **Letters from Prison** – affirmed the Christian life, standing against all things evil. He did not dwell on suffering.

In these he calls on Christians to take a stand against **INJUSTICE**- Jesus was **'the man for others'** and so the Church as Christ's body must also be a Church for others. It was failing.

Sacrifice & Suffering

The Cross embodies the suffering of Christ and in human suffering, Christianity engages with the world reflected in this Cross of suffering.

God, too, suffers in Jesus, acting in solidarity with humankind. The ultimate expression of this is the cry of **DERELICTION** from the **CROSS.**

"My God, My God, why have you forsaken me?" (Mark 15:34, Psalm 22:2)

- **KRISIS** (Barth's use of NT Greek) – judgement, decision, verdict.

- **PARADOX** – God reveals His 'crisis' (judgement, redemption) in response to 'crisis' of the world (sinfulness, injustice, murder etc.)

THEOLOGY OF CRISIS - Crisis of human sinfulness can only be triumphed over by God's **JUDGEMENT** and faith in His redemption through Jesus Christ.

The **Passion of Jesus Christ** – his sufferings leading up to and including his death are linked to the call to **DISCIPLESHIP**. 'Those who would come after me must leave self behind, take up their **CROSS** and follow me!' (Mark 8:34)

Jesus died without admiration or honour, 'a man of **SORROWS** and acquainted with grief' (Isaiah 53).

Being a disciple means 'picking up the cross' and so suffering and sacrifice are an inherent aspect of the nature of discipleship.

Solidarity

Solidarity with the Jews - Bonhoeffer wrote his essay '**The Church and the Jewish Question'** in response to the boycott of Jewish business in April **1933**. Called for solidarity of those afflicted by Nazism.

BONHOEFFER Publicly rejected the claim that punishment of the Jews was God's work for their rejection and death of Christ. He called it **GODLESS VIOLENCE**– in response to **NIGHT OF BROKEN GLASS (KRISTELNACHT) 1938.**

Living the '**Christian life**' is not to 'become religious' but to be there for other people, sharing in their experiences in a form of **TRANSCENDENCE**.

Strengths

1. Bonhoeffer's focus on **SHARED REFLECTION** and reading of Scripture, alongside shared living and community provide a good basis for understanding the Scripture and not just choosing parts of it.

2. A **COMMUNAL** approach could discourage distorted understanding of God's will. Church exist as **SALT** and **LIGHT** for everyone.

3. Bonhoeffer's account of true Christianity and what was wrong with the German Christians being misled by the Nazi-Controlled German Church would

seem **ACCURATE** and attracts sympathy today.

4. Calls into question the nature of civic authorities and what they are doing – Bonhoeffer proposed an **ETHIC OF ACTION**. This action needed to be **COSTLY** - so Christians emerge from the shadows and become visible agents of change.

Weaknesses

1. Interpreting God's will might be **MISTAKEN**. Action that includes violence (as in some forms of **LIBERATION THEOLOGY**) opposed by **MARTIN LUTHER KING**'s theology of **NON-VIOLENT** resistance.

2. It is not always clear how God will want us to act in any given situation - requires God-like **WISDOM.**

3. If someone has a distorted view of God's will, Bonhoeffer's teaching could be **DANGEROUS** and even support genocide as in the book of **JOSHUA** where entire peoples were wiped out in cities of Jericho and Ai.

4. St Paul's Romans 13:1-2 suggests that **OBEDIENCE** to the state is important as state leaders have been established by God. Bonhoeffer differs from this.

5. Even Jesus did not openly challenge the rule of **PONTIUS PILATE** and he did not encourage people not to pay their taxes, even though he did challenge religious authorities and social norms. Contrast with the **ZEALOTS** who fostered a disastrous rebellion against Rome in **66AD** which led directly to the destruction of the Jewish **TEMPLE** in **70AD.**

Possible Exam Questions

1. "Using the will of God as a guide for moral behaviour is impractical, as in most circumstances it is impossible to know what God wants us to do." Discuss.

2. To what extent, if at all, does the theology of Bonhoeffer have relevance for Christians today?

3. "Bonhoeffer's most important teaching is on leadership." Discuss.

4. "Christian ethics means being obedient to God's will." Discuss.

5. To what extent was Bonhoeffer's religious community at Finkenwalde successful?

6. "Costly grace is the key to Bonhoeffer's theology and action". Discuss

Key Quotes

"Whoever wishes to take up the problem of a Christian ethic must ... ask 'what is the will of God?'" Dietrich Bonhoeffer, Ethics, p. 161.

"The nature of this will of God can only be clear in the moment of action"." Dietrich Bonhoeffer, No Rusty Swords, p. 43.

"For the sake of Christ, the worldly order is subject to the commandment of God...There exists, therefore, a Christian responsibility for secular institutions,". Dietrich Bonhoeffer: Ethics (1955/2005), p. 289

"We make again and again the surprising and terrifying discovery that the will of God does not reveal itself before our eyes as clearly as we had hoped." Dietrich Bonhoeffer: No Rusty Swords (1965), p. 46

"And Jesus answering said unto them, Render to Caesar the things that are Caesar's, and to God the things that are God's. And they marvelled at him." Mark 12:17

"Let everyone be subject to the governing authorities, for there is no authority except that which God has established. The authorities that exist have been established by God." Romans 13:1

"Costly because it costs man his life, and it is grace because it gives man the only true life ... Above all, it is costly because it cost God the life of his Son' (The Cost of Discipleship, p. 5).

"There is no road to faith or discipleship, no other road – only obedience to the call of Jesus" (Dietrich Bonhoeffer, The Cost of discipleship, 1959, p. 49)

"The followers are a visible community; their discipleship visible in action which lifts them out of the world" Dietrich Bonhoeffer, The Cost of Discipleship, 1959, p. 106

"Who will speak up for those who are voiceless?" Psalm 31:8

"When Christ calls a man, he bids him come and die...Suffering then, is the badge of true discipleship" (Bonhoeffer, The Cost of Discipleship, 1959, p. 79, p., 80)

Religious Pluralism and Theology

Background

Christianity has always existed alongside other religions. In its growth out of **JUDAISM**, Christians had to decide the extent to which they would continue with beliefs and practices of others, and what was it that was going to make them distinctively Christian. The question of whether other religions contain valuable truths remains, as well as the extent to which Christians can be seen to have a unique **EXCLUSIVE** relationship with God. Issues within religious pluralism and society also arise, for example, should Christians work to convert others or is it possible for non-Christians to achieve salvation too.

Specification

At A level, you will need to explain and evaluate the teaching of contemporary Christian theology of religion on exclusivism, inclusivism, and pluralism. You need to show knowledge and understanding of:

1. The view that only Christianity fully offers the means of salvation

2. The view that although Christianity is the normative means of salvation, 'anonymous' Christians may also receive salvation

3. The view that there are many ways to salvation, of which Christianity is one path (OCR A Level in Religious Studies Specification, 2016, p. 36)

Key Terms

- **EXCLUSIVISM:** the view that only one religion offers the full means of salvation

- **INTER-FAITH DIALOGUE:** discussing religious beliefs between members of different religious traditions, with an intention of reaching better understanding

- **THEOLOGY OF RELIGION:** a branch of Christian theology that considers the relationship between Christianity and other world religions from a Christian perspective

- **INCLUSIVISM:** the view that although one's own religion sets the standard (is 'normative') for means of salvation, those who accept its fundamental principles may also attain salvation

- **PLURALISM:** the view that there are several means of salvation through different religious traditions

- **PARTICULARISM:** another name for exclusivism, meaning that salvation can only be found in one particular way

- **VATICAN II:** the Second Vatican Ecumenical Council, held from 1962 to 1965 to deliberate the place of the Catholic Church in the modern world

- **NOUMENA:** a Kantian term to describe reality as it really is, unaffected by the human mind

- **PHENOMENA:** a Kantian term to describe reality as it seems to us, filtered by the human mind

Structure of Thought - Religious Pluralism

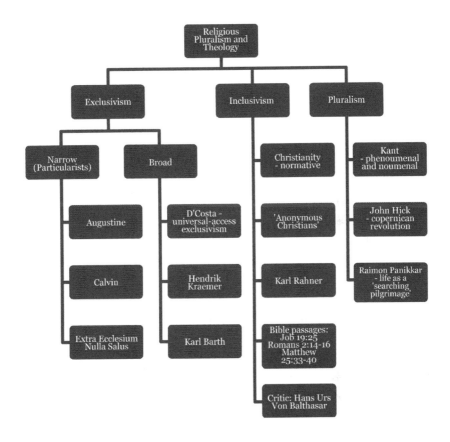

Christian Teaching on Exclusivism

EXCLUSIVISM is the belief that only Christianity offers the means of salvation. It comes from the belief that Jesus is 'the' way, not 'a' way to salvation. Another word for exclusivism is **PARTICULARIST**.

Christ's **SACRIFICE** was **UNIQUE**. Salvation can only reach those who hear the gospel and respond to this with faith. A sign of this acceptance is **BAPTISM**.

NARROW EXCLUSIVISM is the belief that salvation is possible only for those of a particular Christian denomination (Baptist, Catholic, Lutheran, Anglican). **AUGUSTINE** and **CALVIN** are examples of **PARTICULARISTS**. They believed God only elects – through grace - a small number of Christians for salvation. **Catholics** believe there is no salvation outside of the Church – **EXTRA ECCLESIAM NULLA SALUS**. The Catholic view has been considered less narrow since **LUMEN GENTIUM** – "many elements of sanctification and of truth are found outside of its visible structure" (1964).

BROAD EXCLUSIVISM is the belief that salvation is possible for all who accept Christ, regardless of denomination. Other religions may contain some truth, but not enough for salvation. Gavin **D'COSTA** asserted **UNIVERSAL-ACCESS EXCLUSIVISM** – that salvation is possible after death. **1 TIMOTHY 2:3-4** supports this – "this is good, and pleases God our Saviour, who wants all people to be saved and to come to a knowledge of the truth".

HENDRIK KRAEMER – The Christian Message in a Non-Christian World. Kraemer was part of the **ECUMENICAL MOVEMENT** aiming to bring different Christian denominations together. Worked among missionaries in non-Christian countries, spreading the message that salvation could only be achieved by converting to Christianity. We should evaluate religions

HOLISTICALLY to see if 'as a whole', the religion accepts Christ's salvation or not.

KARL BARTH – Church Dogmatics. Emphasised the importance of Christ for salvation. Humans cannot achieve salvation on their own. Presents **'THEOLOGY OF THE WORD'** – God can only be known where He chooses to reveal this knowledge through His Word – through Christ's life, death, and resurrection; through the Bible and through Church teaching. Revelation is always God's choice. **CHRIST** is the **FULLY UNIQUE** way God has chosen to reveal himself and so is the only fully reliable way of gaining knowledge of God.

Christian Teaching on Inclusivism

INCLUSIVISM is a middle path between exclusivism and pluralism. Christianity is a **NORMATIVE** means of salvation but **'ANONYMOUS'** Christians may also receive salvation (Karl **RAHNER**).

Salvation can be reached by people who turn to Christ in the **AFTERLIFE**. Salvation is possible for those who follow God sincerely, albeit in a wrong religious context. Truth in other religions could be from Christ – even if they do not recognise this.

KARL RAHNER – Christianity sets the **STANDARD** by which other religions should be measured. An **OMNIBENEVOLENT** God should be able to offer salvation to those who have not been able to freely accept Christ. Christianity holds the truth, but people can follow Christ unknowingly. People who do not know Christ can still have a relationship with God – e.g. **JOB 19:25**. Such people are called **ANONYMOUS CHRISTIANS**.

HENDRIK KRAEMER - disagreed with Rahner. **NON-CHRISTIAN RELIGIONS** were **CULTURAL CONSTRUCTS**, not responses to God's revelation through Christ.

The **BIBLE** can be seen as a source of authority:

1. **JOB 19:25** – Job appears to refer to Jesus – "I know that my redeemer lives".

2. **ROMANS 2:14-16** – non-believers can have an innate sense for Christ, even if they do not recognise it – "They show that the requirements of the law are written on their hearts".

3. **MATTHEW 25:33-40** – the Parable of the Sheep and the Goats implies anyone living by altruistic love is working for Christ – whether they realise it or not. "What you do for the least person, you do for me" says Jesus.

HANS URS VON BALTHASAR – **CRITIC** of the '**ANONYMOUS CHRISTIAN**'. Multi-culturalism should not be an excuse to 'water down' the importance of Christ's crucifixion and resurrection.

Christian Teaching on Pluralism

PLURALISM is the view that there are many ways to salvation. Christianity is one of these. Human culture causes differences in beliefs and practices, but religions share the same ultimate goal.

KANT – there is a difference between the **NOUMENAL WORLD** (world as it really is) and the **PHENOMENAL WORLD** (world as it appears to us). Nature of God belongs to the noumenal world.

JOHN HICK – called for a '**COPERNICAN REVOLUTION**' in theology: to put God central – not Christianity. This call **AWAY FROM** a **CHRISTOCENTRIC** approach to theology is driven by our observations of the world, just as the **COSMOLOGICAL COPERNICAN REVOLUTION** was.

Religion is a **PHENOMENAL** attempt to understand God (by experience). All religions fall short of the truth. Christianity's 'truth claims' e.g. Virgin Birth, should be understood as myths expressing human relationship with 'the **REAL'**. God is **BENEVOLENT** and so salvation must be extended to all.

Hick's call for **DEMYTHOLOGIZATION** of the Bible has origins in **RUDOLF BULTMANN**. This is the idea that the Gospels do contain essential truths but these are revealed through **MYTHS**.

Hick argues it is impossible to create rational arguments for God e.g. **NATURAL THEOLOGY**. People are given reason to believe by **RELIGIOUS EXPERIENCES**. Knowledge of God is similar to our other knowledge of the world – through our experiences. Since individual experiences provide the grounding for belief, we must respect all religions, since none of them can provide universally-accepted argument for their beliefs. Experiences of God can be interpreted through the lens of different religions and faith is how we interpret these events. An **ANALOGY** is how different people respond differently to the same **MUSICAL STIMULUS**, influenced by their cultural background. Cultural influences might explain the differences in how people interpret the divine. Human projection shapes the experience but does not cause it.

Challenges to Pluralism

Supporting Hick

- **FEUERBACH -** religious belief is projection. No genuine external cause of the religious experience

- **CUPITT -** challenges existence of God

- **PHILOSOPHICAL ARGUMENTS** – if 'the Real' is unknowable, we can't say anything meaningful about it and it cannot reveal itself deliberately to humans – this would make the revelation come from the human mind.

- Hick's theology allows for a **GLOBAL** theology and does not exclude polytheistic or non-theistic religions

Opposing Hick

- **INCARNATION** is regarded as central to Christianity, affirmed in the creed. Hick challenges traditional doctrines.

- **CHRISTIANS** might argue Hick undermines the essence of Christianity and reduces the Bible to fiction with morals.

- **LEE STROBEL** – 'the Case for Christ' – the gospels are eyewitness documents. But we know very little of Jesus' early life and the gospels were written after Jesus' death.

CONCLUSION OF HICK's PLURALISTIC HYPOTHESIS Empirical evidence, practical considerations and philosophical logic lend themselves to a Copernican revolution in theology.

How Was Hick Influenced by Kant?

The distinction between **NOUMENA** and **PHENOMENA** helps us to comprehend how different religions are talking about the same reality (noumena) but do so in different ways since our mind shapes our perception of our experiences (phenomena).

SYNOPTIC connection **PLATO** (Forms) -> **KANT** (noumena) -> **HICK**

RAIMON PANIKKAR – we need to be 'open' about the truth, rather than making claims about it. Life is a **'SEARCHING PILGRIMAGE'** and we might need to let go of traditions in order to find our identity. **CHRISTOPHANY** is God's way of making Himself known to people. **RELIGIOUS PLURALISM** is a **SPIRITUAL POSITION** not an intellectual position.

Confusions to Avoid

1. Hick is NOT calling for one religion with everyone having the same beliefs – **GLOBAL THEOLOGY** is NOT the same as a **GLOBAL RELIGION**. He is emphasising that people necessarily have different ways of experiencing the divine.

2. Hick is NOT saying all religions are correct – rather, that they **CONTAIN TRUTH**. They also contain human projection and error and since we cannot know all truth, we must respect all religions.

3. For the belief system to be valid, it ought to lead people away from selfishness and towards ethical living. Therefore, not every belief system reflects the Divine.

Possible Exam Questions

1. "A theologically pluralist approach significantly undermines the central doctrines of Christianity." Discuss.

2. To what extent can non-Christians who live morally good lives and genuinely seek God be considered to be 'anonymous Christians'?

3. Critically assess the view that only Christianity offers the means of salvation

4. "Christianity is one of many ways to salvation." Discuss.

Key Quotes

"Those also can attain to salvation who through no fault of their own do not know the Gospel of Christ or His Church, yet sincerely seek God and moved by grace strive by their deeds to do His will as it is known to them through the dictates of conscience". (Catechism, paragraph 19)

"I know that my redeemer lives, and that in the end he will stand on the earth" Job 19:25

"All that matters (metaphysically) is that Jesus did rise from the dead, and that this act made salvation possible for all, irrespective of one's particular religion." (Religion, Key Concepts in Philosophy, 2007, p. 154)

"This is good, and pleases God our Saviour, who wants all people to be saved and to come to a knowledge of the truth". (1 Timothy 2:3-4)

"They show that the requirements of the law are written on their hearts".
(Romans 2:14-16)

"Whoever believes in him is not condemned, but whoever does not believe stands condemned already because they have not believed in the name of God's one and only Son." (John 3:18)

"For it is by grace you have been saved, through faith—and this is not from yourselves, it is the gift of God— 9 not by works, so that no one can boast." (Ephesians 2:8-9)

"You see that a person is considered righteous by what they do and not by faith alone." (James 2:24)

Suggested Reading

Hick's official website:
http://www.johnhick.org.uk/jsite/index.php/articles-by-john-hick

Philosopher Kings website:
http://www.philosopherkings.co.uk/hickandpluralism.html

Hick, J. (1995) God and the Universe of Faiths, SCM Press, Chapters 1 and 10

McGrath, A. (2010 5th Edition) A Christian Theology, Wiley-Blackwell, Chapter 17

D'Costa, G. (2009) Christianity and World Religions, Wiley-Blackwell

Religious Pluralism and Society

Background

In the 21st Century, a question that concerns many Christians is how they relate to people who follow no religion, or non-Christian beliefs. This goes together with the **MULTI-CULTURALISM** of Britain, leading it to become a multi-faith society. Issues arise for a Christian who might ask themselves whether to tolerate, or try to convert other people. Issues of religious expression in the workplace and attitudes towards sexuality have also made the public eye in the media. Christians might be unsure of how to voice their opinion without being discriminatory. Some Christians have become involved in **INTER-FAITH DIALOGUE**.

Specification

At A level, you will need to explain and evaluate:

1. The development of contemporary **MULTI-FAITH** societies – the reasons for this development, for example, migration

2. Christian responses to, including:

a. Responses of Christian communities to inter-faith dialogue

b. The scriptural reasoning movement (its methods and aims; and how the mutual study and interpretation of different religions' sacred literature can help understanding of different and conflicting religious truth claims)

3. How Christian communities have responded to the challenge of encounters with other faiths, for example:

a. Catholic Church: **REDEMPTORIS MISSIO (ENCYCLICAL**, pp. 55-57)

b. Church of England: Sharing the Gospel of Salvation (OCR A Level in Religious Studies Specification, 2016, p. 37)

Key Terms

- **ENCYCLICAL** an open letter sent by the Catholic hierarchy to the churches, endorsed by the Pope

- **MISSIONARY WORK** activity that aims to convert people to a particular faith or set of beliefs, or works for social justice in areas of poverty or deprivation

- **MULTI-FAITH SOCIETIES** societies in which there are significant populations of people with different religious beliefs

- **SOCIAL COHESION** when a group is united by bonds that help them to live together peacefully

- **SYNOD** the legislative body of the Church of England

Structure of Thought - Pluralism and Society

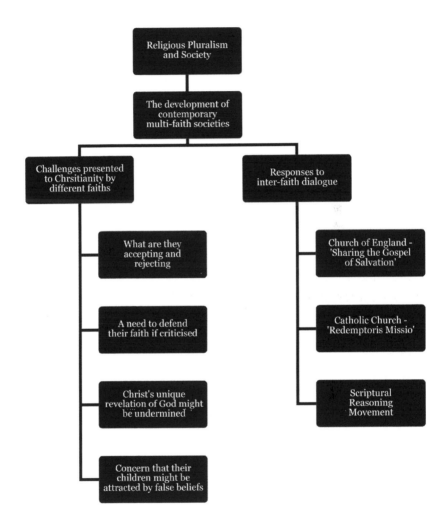

The Development of Multi-Faith Societies

Example - Migration

Christianity was introduced by the **ROMANS**. Before this, religious practices concentrated around worship of ancestors, fertility and agriculture. Christianity was established as the **PRIMARY FAITH** in Britain in **7th CENTURY**. Western development in **TRAVEL** and **COMMUNICATION** has increased **CULTURAL** and **RELIGIOUS DIVERSITY**. In the 1950s and 60s, the Textile industry was short of labour - encouraging immigration from **PAKISTAN** and the **CARIBBEAN**. **IDI AMIN** expelled the **ASIAN** population from **UGANDA** in 1972. This led to arrival in Britain of **HINDUS, MUSLIMS** and **SIKHS.**

People have travelled more for holiday and work and this has led to greater contact with different beliefs and traditions. 'Pockets' of religious groups were caused by religious people choosing to live near where others who practised the same religion. **SIKHS** arriving in 1950s for work tended to settle in **LONDON, BIRMINGHAM** and **WEST YORKSHIRE**; while the **JEWISH** population is higher in **NORTH LONDON** and **LEEDS**. When travelling, local etiquette needs respecting and for this, further education about beliefs is also needed.

MAX MULLER'S 19th century translations of Hindu texts into English (**THE SACRED BOOKS OF THE EAST**) increased interest in meditation and ideas such as **REINCARNATION**.

The changes have resulted in **MIXED-FAITH MARRIAGES,** the teaching of world faiths in schools, people working among **RELIGIOUS DIVERSITY**, the stocking of multi-faith **FESTIVAL FOODS** in supermarkets, **PRAYER ROOMS** in airports and hospitals, and an acceptance of **ATHEISM** and

AGNOSTICISM, allowing religious beliefs to also be challenged.

Some argue that this new opportunity for the sharing of beliefs has helped to dispel prejudice and to **PROMOTE PEACE**. Others say it has helped **DEEPER REFLECTION** on one's own beliefs; while others still, claim tolerance is promoted at the expense of the **UNIQUE MESSAGE** of **SALVATION** through **CHRIST** promoted by the Christian mission.

Responses to Inter-faith Dialogue

Inter-faith dialogue is also known as inter-belief dialogue and inter-religious dialogue. It aims for mutual peace, respect, and cooperation. It aims to understand:

• Common ground and points of difference

• One's own faith while learning about, and from, beliefs of others

It is NOT about **CONVERSION** but serves renewed interest in the wake of migration and human responses to tragedies such 9/11.

David Ford: The Future of Christian Theology

Inter-faith dialogue has new direction due to two major historical strands:

1. **HOLOCAUST**: the role played by Christianity in spurring on anti-Semitism in contrast with those that opposed Nazism. **DABRU EMET ('SPEAK THE TRUTH')** – was an invitation from Jewish leaders to Christians, calling for

CO-OPERATION.

2. Rising **TENSIONS** between Islam and the West: **A COMMON WORD BETWEEN US AND YOU** – a call from Muslim leaders to Christianity outlining the responsibility of both to work for the common good of all.

Catholic Church - Redemptoris Missio (Mission of the Redeemer)

JOHN PAUL II – encouraged perseverance with the Christian mission in a multi-faith world. **PAPAL ENCYCLICALS** – letters from the Pope to Church leaders, are considered to be an authority and a 'final word.' **REDEMPTORIS MISSIO** (1990) re-visited the issues of **VATICAN II** and affirmed the essential place of Christian mission in a multi-faith world.

All religions provide spiritual opportunity, despite gaps and errors. The **LAITY** understand Christianity as lived through everyday life and so have a key role in dialogue.

All **CATHOLICS** have a duty to engage in **RESPECTFUL DIALOGUE**. This dialogue gives an opportunity to bear witness and is an 'expression' of Christian mission – not an opposition to it. The unique path to salvation through Christ is still offered by Christianity and should be emphasised.

Church of England - Sharing the Gospel of Salvation

1. 'THE DIALOGUE OF DAILY LIFE' – informal discussions of differing beliefs

2. 'THE DIALOGUE OF THE COMMON GOOD' – different faiths cooperate to help the community

3. 'THE DIALOGUE OF MUTUAL UNDERSTANDING' – formal debates e.g. Scriptural Reasoning

4. **'THE DIALOGUE OF SPIRITUAL LIFE'** – meet for prayer and worship

This **FOURFOLD PLAN** to **SHARING THE GOSPEL OF SALVATION** is in response to **PAUL EDDY'S** 2006 question asking the Church to clarify the position of the Church of England on converting others. The plan affirmed that Jesus uniquely offers salvation and the Church of England has a mission to testify to this.

Christians should make efforts to speak about their beliefs openly and honestly but should not treat this as a 'marketing' exercise. Conversions are God's work – not the result of a 'good sell'.

Christians should make efforts to engage with members of different faiths – **MORE THAN JUST TOLERANCE.** Christians should follow the **GOLDEN RULE** – to 'treat others as you would like to be treated' (**LEVITICUS 19:18**) and should listen to others and leave judgement to God.

The Scriptural Reasoning Movement

How the mutual study and interpretation of different religions' sacred literature can help understanding of different and conflicting religious truth claims.

The movement began as a **JEWISH ACADEMIC FORUM** in the USA. In the mid-1990s, Christians asked to join to learn and found the conversations to be engaging. **MUSLIMS** were asked to join because of shared roots (**COMMON GROUND**) and together, the three religions can be known as **RELIGIONS OF THE BOOK** because each religion claims to have a holy text that is authoritative and revelatory. The movement now welcomes people of **ALL FAITHS**.

Cambridge Inter-faith Forum

This involves a discussion of themes considering scriptures of the Abrahamic faiths (those that come from a common origin in the **HEBREW** Scriptures) – Judaism, Christianity, Islam. Discussions are held in English in order to be inclusive. Discussions will concern earning, clothing, modesty, fasting, differing truth claims (e.g. Prophethood and Trinity) among other topics. The forum will consider how beliefs that appear similar are understood in their own contexts. Honesty and openness are encouraged.

Strengths

Brings together people of different faiths, aiding **TOLERANCE** in a multi-faith society.

IDEAS - Collaboration socially and academically is encouraged.

Face-to-face discussion is encouraged, as well as joint research. This further promotes inter-religious harmony and **SOCIAL COHESION** through raised awareness and understanding of one's own views and those of others.

Weaknesses

INDIVIDUALISTIC - Participants represent themselves – it is possible we lose sight of the normative teaching of each religion.

It is difficult to decide if an interpretation is **REASONABLE**.

It is **QUESTIONABLE** – the extent to which theological **EXCLUSIVISTS** can engage fully in inter-faith dialogue.

Although open to all faiths, the extent to which non-Abrahamic faiths with varied origins and traditions can partake fully and benefit, is questionable.

Some will criticise the **RELATIVIZING** of religious groups by treating all beliefs as equally valid.

Confusions to Avoid

1. There is some debate as to whether conversion of those of no faith is significantly different to conversion of those of a previous faith. On the one hand, those converting from a previous faith might face bigger challenges because of their **FAMILY** and social group.

2. This tension might not be the same for someone of no religious background – thought, their social group might change. On the other hand, some **INCLUSIVISTS** might argue that the non-religious have a greater need to

know God than the 'anonymous Christian' does. The non-religious might never have encountered the opportunity to become religious; while others might have actively opposed religion.

Possible Exam Questions

1. To what extent should Christians seek to convert others to Christianity at every opportunity?

2. "Inter-faith dialogue is of little practical use." Discuss.

3. To what extent does scriptural reasoning relativise religious beliefs?

4. "Converting people of no faith should be equally important to a Christian as converting people of non-Christian faith." Discuss.

Key Quotations

From Redemptoris Missio (paragraphs) and the Bible:

"Every person has the right to hear the 'Good News' of the God who reveals and gives himself in Christ" Para. 46

"In the light of the economy of salvation, the Church sees no conflict between proclaiming Christ and engaging in inter-faith dialogue" Para. 55

"The Church gladly acknowledges whatever is true and holy in the religious traditions of Buddhism, Hinduism and Islam as a reflection of that truth which enlightens all people" Para. 55

"Dialogue should be conducted and implemented with the conviction that the Church is the ordinary means of salvation and that she alone possesses the fullness of the means of salvation" Para. 55

"Dialogue leads to inner purification and conversion" Para. 56

"Inter-religious dialogue is a part of the church's evangelising mission" Para. 55

"Therefore go and make disciples of all nations, baptising them in the names of the Father and of the Son and of the Holy Spirit." (Matthew 28:19)

Suggested Reading

The Doctrine Commission of the Church of England (1995) The Mystery of Salvation Church House Publishing, Chapter 7

Ford, D. (2011) The Future of Christian Theology, Wiley-Blackwell, Chapter 7

Pope Paul VI (1965) Nostra Aetate; Declaration on the relation of the Church to non-Christian religions

The Challenge of Secularism

Background

The role of religion in Western Europe has changed and is changing. Christianity in Britain has been in decline – seen in Church attendance and solemnisation of fewer marriages. This reduction has led to questions from **PSYCHOLOGY** and **SOCIOLOGY** about the role of religious institutions in public life and culture. It has been suggested that religion should be seen as part of the '**PRIVATE**' rather than 'public' sphere while the relationship between Christianity and British culture is diminishing.

Specification

At A level, you will need to explain the rise of **SECULARISM** and **SECULARISATION**, and know and evaluate:

1. The views that God is an illusion and the result of wish fulfilment

2. The views of Freud and Dawkins that society would be happier without Christianity as it is infantile, repressive and causes conflict

3. The views that Christianity should play no part in public life

4. The views of **SECULAR HUMANISTS** that Christian belief is personal and should play no part in public life, including education and schools, and government and state (OCR A Level in Religious Studies Specification, 2016, p. 40). Be aware that there are two different approaches to secularism, and one of these argues that **SECULARISM** is absolutely necessary for religious

toleration and diversity, (the other, argued by **DAWKINS**, argues that religion should be completely excluded form public life).

Key Terms

- **SECULAR** not connected or associated with religious or spiritual matters

- **SECULARISM** various meanings – a belief that religion should have no role in public or government life; a belief that no one religion should have a superior position in the state; a belief in a public space and a private space, and that religion should be kept apart from public power

- **SECULARISATION** a theory rising out of Enlightenment thinking, developed in the 1950s and 1960s, that proposed that with the advancement of democracy and technology, religious belief would progressively decline. Such a linear decline is now doubted by sociologists

- **WISH FULFILMENT** according to Freud, the satisfaction of a desire through a dream or other exercise of the imagination

Structure of Thought - Challenge of Secularism

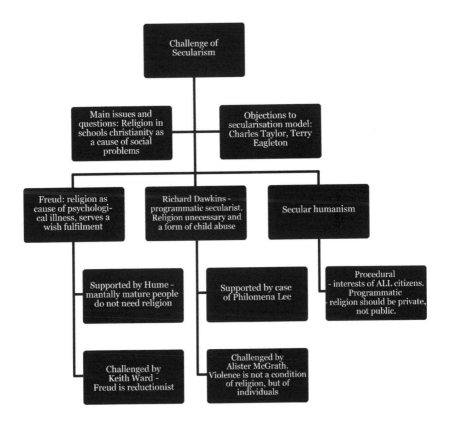

The Rise of Secularism and Secularisation

Important Aims to Understand

1. Reasons for the rise of secularism and secularisation and the views that God is an illusion and the result of wish fulfilment

2. The views of Freud and Dawkins that society would be happier without Christianity as it is infantile, repressive and causes conflict

Difficulty in Defining Secularism

1. Measuring and defining terms: less Church attendance does not mean less spirituality

2. Influence and authority: new movements are being accepted by society, even with a decline in mainstream religions

3. Religious commitment and evidence of the past: Church attendance in previous years was not the best test of religious commitment. Today, people attend because they want to, not because they must. So, what really is an appropriate way of measuring secularisation?

AUGUSTE COMPTE - civilised society develops progressively from:

1. *Theological* perspective

2. *Metaphysical* (abstract) view of the world

3. *Positive* (scientific/rational) view of the world

Sigmund Freud

Religion is a key cause of **PSYCHOLOGICAL** illness. Tradition and conformity **REPRESS** natural instincts, and this leads to **NEUROSES**.

Freud considered that religion belongs to the **INFANTILE** – belief is formed in the early stage of human social development. This stage is before the person has developed the ability to reason and at this stage, needs external care and security provided by a **FATHER** and **MOTHER** figure (by **PROJECTION**, God and the Virgin Mary).

Supported by Hume

Mentally mature people do not need religion – it is practised by the uneducated.

Freud went further to say that religion was a **SICKNESS** and could be proven as such by his use of psychoanalysis.

When instinctual life wins and religion ends, humans will be content.

Wish Fulfilment

As children, there is a **VULNERABILITY** and helplessness that is fulfilled 'by a belief that injustices will be corrected, that life has a purpose, and that there is a moral code' (Freud, The Future of an Illusion). God – or belief in God – represents a **PERSONIFICATION** of our needs. Religion can answer questions that humans have that cannot be answered by studying 'what is real?'

Religion causes conflict as it creates unreliable and harmful answers to human uncertainty and matters outside of our control.

Challenges to Freud

KEITH WARD labels Freud a **REDUCTIONIST** because he appears to reduce everything to material terms. This is an **INADEQUATE** explanation for the spiritual experience of existence.

Truth claims about religion cannot be disproved.

Freud emphasises the **DESTRUCTIVE** nature of religion but for others, religion is an aide rather than a harm. It can assist understanding and acceptance of life. Religion can help to form communities rather than to divide them.

Freud **GENERALISES** religions – while some are hierarchical and controlling, not all are and therefore, not all religions can be seen to perpetuate guilt.

Wish fulfilment might not always lead to illusion – it can lead to creativity such as that seen in **DREAMS** and daydreams.

Richard Dawkins - Programmatic Secularism

In **THE GOD DELUSION**, Dawkins makes the case for:

1. Imagining a world without religion

2. Accepting that the God hypothesis is weak

3. Realising that religion is a form of child abuse

4. Accepting atheism with pride

Dawkins argued that life can be meaningful without reference to religion. The processes of nature can be most clearly explained by Charles Darwin and his **THEORY** of **EVOLUTION**.

Belief in God is **DELUDED** and unnecessary. Religion is delusional since it represents a persistent false belief going against the main body of evidence. The supernatural world cannot be subject to empirical study and therefore, Dawkins rejects **STEPHEN JAY GOULD'S** attempts to argue that religion and science are '**NON-OVERLAPPING MAGISTERIA**'. For Dawkins, all things must be able to be studied empirically. (Link with **VERIFICATIONISM** in Religious Language).

RELIGION IS A FORM OF CHILD ABUSE – A child lacking understanding should not be labelled as religious. Dawkins criticised the state for allowing a child below the age of consent and reason to be labelled as religious. They have been unable to think about the beliefs they are labelled as possessing. This could be seen in school admissions, for example.

Dawkins used the example of **CATHOLICISM** as a form of long-term psychological abuse. He gave the example of Catholic women who had experienced sexual abuse, who found the fear of hell to be greater than the abuse itself. Another example was the '**HELL HOUSE**' thought of by a pastor in Colorado. Here, children were terrified by actors role-playing the sins of abortion and homosexuality, followed by the torture of Hell. Dawkins suggests that the power of belief in religion becomes greater than the physical abuse suffered.

Example- Philomena Lee

Had her child, born out of wedlock, taken from her by the Catholic Church. She stayed with her boy for three years at the **SEAN ROSS ABBEY** in Roscrea – a place for unwed mothers. Philomena's boy was then sold, to be adopted by a

Catholic family.

Responses to Dawkins - Alister McGrath

The Dawkins Delusion

Many Christians think faith is not irrational. Furthermore, religion and science are not necessarily in conflict. Science can explain the intelligible universe and so **DAWKINS** is right to criticise the **'GOD OF THE GAPS'**. However, the intelligible universe could still point to an intelligent designer.

The relationship between science and religion can be **COMPLEMENTARY**, reflecting different aspects of human experience.

Dawkins' **LIMITED POSITIVIST VIEW** that metaphysical questions are outside of scientific enquiry and therefore meaningless is criticised by many scientists. Science, theology and philosophy can provide useful insights.

MCGRATH also criticised Dawkins' claim that violence was a necessary condition of religion. Jesus taught against violence – "turn the other cheek". Violence is a condition of certain individuals, not religion as a whole. McGrath also notes that atheism has also been a part of violence and repression, e.g. in communist regimes.

Secular Humanism - Christian Belief is Personal

Two Types of Secularism

1. **PROCEDURAL**: the interests of ALL citizens – religious and non-religious,

should be considered by the state. Religion should be treated equally to other institutions but not with preference.

2. **PROGRAMMATIC**: in a **PLURAL** society, the state should be solely secular. This means religious views and practices should be kept apart from public institutions – schools, universities, public holiday and government.

The main aims of modern humanism were set out in the **AMSTERDAM DECLARATION** of 1952:

1. Humanism is **ETHICAL**: all humans are of worth, have dignity and autonomy

2. Humanism is **RATIONAL**: science should be used imaginatively and as a basis for solving human difficulties.

3. Humanism supports democracy and human **RIGHTS**: the best way in which humans can develop their potential.

4. Humanism insists that personal **LIBERTY** must be combined with **SOCIAL RESPONSIBILITY**: no dogmatic beliefs, the autonomous person has a responsibility to society and the natural world

5. Humanism is a response to the widespread demand for an alternative to dogmatic religion: continuous observation will build our reliable understanding of the world and revision of **SCIENTIFIC** understanding.

6. Humanism values artistic **CREATIVITY** and imagination: enhancing human existence. Novelist **E.M. FORSTER** defined the humanist as someone with "curiosity, a free mind, belief in good taste, and belief in the human race."

7. Humanism is a **LIFESTANCE** aiming at the maximum possible fulfilment: creative and ethical living can help us to achieve the challenges of the present

Education and Schools

Government and State

1776 – Formation of the USA – Church and State made separate.

Keeping Church and State separate might be seen as one way of avoiding conflicting political aims between Christian denominations and even with other religions with the increase in migrants.

Alternative ideas about theocracy are seen in:

1. **DOMINIONISTS**: America should be ruled according to Biblical laws – based on Genesis 1:28 where humans are said to have dominion – this includes over the state. A view held mostly by Protestant, evangelical and conservative groups.

2. **RECONSTRUCTIONISTS**: Similar Dominionist notion. Seen in the Old Testament when the life of Israel was ordered according to laws given to Moses. Followed by Calvinists.

In England, the Queen is the Head of the Church of England. 26 Bishops sit as **'LORDS SPIRITUAL'** in the **HOUSE OF LORDS**. Regardless of faith, church of England Parish Churches can be used for marriages, funerals and baptisms. This is a way of the state providing a spiritual life for everyone.

NOTE: England is NOT a **THEOCRACY.**

Some **PROGRAMMATIC SECULARISTS** believe the government should go further in separating Church and State.

ROWAN WILLIAMS – the Church has a role to play in resisting the apparent threat of secularism felt by some religious fundamentalists who are anti-democratic (as they oppose democratic consensus on laws such as legalisation of abortion and homosexuality reform)

CHRISTOPHER DAWSON – secular education systems bring challenges. They deprive people of the ability and right to make sense of their own culture – a culture which, to a large extent, is immersed in religion.

Objections to the Secularisation Model

CHARLES TAYLOR – the '**SUBTRACTION STORIES**' of **DAWKINS** and **FREUD** show how the world can be explained with stories that show neither God, nor any 'greater being' is needed for us to live fulfilled lives.

This is '**SELF-SUFFICING HUMANISM**'. This humanism fails because it emphasises the individual and in so doing, loses the **COMMUNAL** aspect of society (notice though, a counter-argument, that humanists argue for **SOCIAL RESPONSIBILITY**). Rather than a discovery that God does not exist, our exclusion of God from our explanation of the world reflects a **WESTERN PHASE**. In order to live a full life, we need to embrace a sense of the divine and distance ourselves from secularism.

TERRY EAGLETON – a **MARXIST** and **CHRISTIAN** approach. Marxist in the sense that he thought it wrong to exclude religious imagination and its contribution to human existence. Eagleton thought the harm of religion should be weighed up against its positive contributions.

The **SPIRITUAL** aspect of human experience can be captured by religion, but not by secularism. People have been prepared to make ultimate sacrifices for truths about existence but not for **AESTHETIC** reasons e.g. sport/ music.

Secularist privatisation has seemed to make religion and morality irrelevant. 9/11 showed the dangers of a **POSITIVIST** view of the world without religion where dangerous extremists interpret the Western secularists as trying to turn the world anti-religious.

Key Confusions to Avoid

1. The discussion concerning whether spiritual values are just 'human values' can sometimes lead to confusion. To say spiritual values are just 'human', implies that there is '**NO SIGNIFICANT OTHER**' to which they are directed or from which they come.

2. Arguments to support this include the belief that values often labelled as 'Christian' are actually fundamental values of being human and part of flourishing in society. Such values include those of **COMPASSION, FORGIVENESS, JUSTICE, AND PEACE**. Furthermore, those who argue that these spiritual values are no different to 'being human', might add that the aforementioned values do not require a belief in God or an afterlife in order to be endorsed.

3. On the other hand, there are arguments that spiritual values are much more than simply 'human'. For example, some spiritual values such as self-sacrifice and 'love your enemies' do not always benefit the human. Spiritual values are untainted by human, material desires, and express a commitment to something 'other'. Furthermore, it has been suggested that the **UNIVERSAL DECLARATION OF HUMAN RIGHTS** is based on the belief that humans have 'ultimate worth', and so values are **ABSOLUTE**.

4. Lastly, there is an argument that human and spiritual values cannot be made separate and this was shown in the **INCARNATION**.

Possible Exam Questions

1. "Christianity has a negative impact on society." Discuss.

2. To what extent are Christian values more than just basic human values?

3. "Christianity should play no part in public life." Discuss.

4. Critically assess the claims that God is an illusion and the result of wish fulfilment.

Key Quotes

"Faith is the root of freedom and programmatic secularism cannot deliver anything comparable". Rowan Williams, Faith in the Public Square, 2012, page 32

"9/11 highlights two extremes of anxiety: faithless Western secular atheism and its fear of religion (and hence its reaction as the 'war on terror') and faithful religious fundamentalism and its fear of positivism, capitalism and secularisation". Michael Wilcockson, Religious studies for A Level Year 2, 2017, page 277

"No, our science is no illusion. But an illusion it would be to suppose that what science cannot give us we can get elsewhere". Sigmund Freud, The Future of an Illusion, 2001, page 56

"The presence or absence of a creative super-intelligence is unequivocally a scientific question". Richard Dawkins, The God Delusion,

2006, page 59

"Dawkins' naïve view that atheists would never carry out crimes in the names of atheism simply founders on the cruel rocks of reality". Alister McGrath and Joanna Collicutt McGrath, The Dawkins Delusion?, 2007, page 78

"There is something infantile in the presumption that somebody else (parents in the case of children, God in the case of adults) has a responsibility to give your life meaning and point." Richard Dawkins, The God Delusion, 2006, p. 404

"The religions of mankind must be classed as among the mass delusions". Sigmund Freud, Civilisation and its Discontents, 1930, page 81

"Children, I'll argue, have a human right not to have their minds crippled by exposure to other people's bad ideas". Nicholas Humphrey, 'What Shall We Tell the Children?' Amnesty Lecture, 21 February 1997,

Suggested Reading

British Humanist Society, https://humanism.org.uk/

Dawkins, R. The God Delusion, Chapter 9

Dawson, C. (1956) 'The Challenge of Secularism' in Catholic World, also online: http://www.catholiceducation.org/en/education/catholic-contributions/the-challenge-of-secularism.html

Ford, D. (2011) The Future of Christian Theology, Wiley-Blackwell, Chapters 3 and 6

Freud, S. The Future of an Illusion

Liberation Theology and Marx

Background

Marx introduced the idea that when humans are unable to live fulfilling lives due to being 'dehumanised', this results in a form of **ALIENATION**. Humans are **DEHUMANISED** when they are **EXPLOITED,** and this is a result of being treated as objects and used as a means to an end.

Marx's teachings on alienation and exploitation have been used by **LIBERATION THEOLOGY** to analyse the **'STRUCTURAL'** causes of **SOCIAL SIN** that have led to poverty, violence, and injustice. Such 'structural' causes include capitalism and institutions (schools, churches, and the state).

The analysis of structural sin has led to a call for the **'PREFERENTIAL OPTION FOR THE POOR'** – a thought calling for Christians to act in solidarity with the poor, rooted in the Gospel. The implication of this teaching is to place **ORTHOPRAXIS** (right action) before **ORTHODOXY** (official Church teaching).

Specification

At A Level, we explain and evaluate liberation theology and Marx, including:

1. Marx's teaching on **ALIENATION** and exploitation

2. **LIBERATION THEOLOGY**'s use of Marx to analyse social sin

3. Liberation theology on the **'PREFERENTIAL OPTION** for the poor'

Key Terms

- **ALIENATION:** The process of becoming detached or isolated

- **BASIC CHRISTIAN COMMUNITIES:** Christian groups that gather to try to directly resolve problems in their lives

- **CAPITALISM:** An economic system in which the means of production are privately owned and operated for profit, in contrast with communism where the state controls trade and industry

- **ORTHODOXY:** Right belief

- **ORTHOPRAXIS**: Right action

- **PREFERENTIAL OPTION FOR THE POOR:** Acting in solidarity with the poor and oppressed

- **STRUCTURAL SIN:** Social dimension of sin, beyond individual sin. It is an attitude of society that contributes to oppression

idea that education is simply about moving information from one generation to the next, he wants it to transform society

" When I give food to the poor they call me a saint. When I ask why have the poor, no food they call me a Communist.'

Dom Helder Camara,
Brazilian Archbishop

Structure of Thought - Liberation Theology and Marx

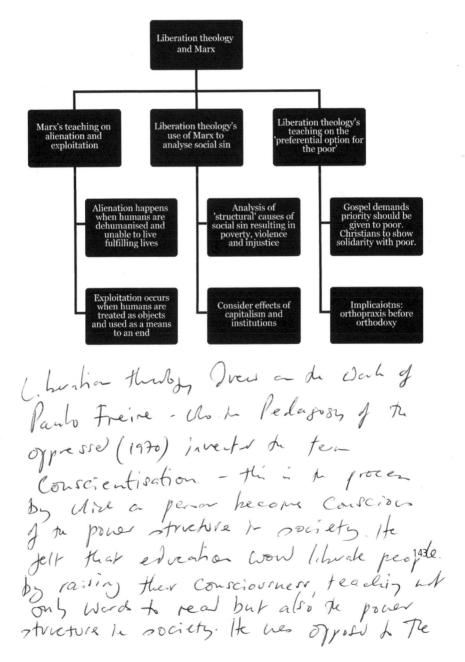

Liberation theology and Marx

- Marx's teaching on alienation and exploitation
  - Alienation happens when humans are dehumanised and unable to live fulfilling lives
  - Exploitation occurs when humans are treated as objects and used as a means to an end
- Liberation theology's use of Marx to analyse social sin
  - Analysis of 'structural' causes of social sin resulting in poverty, violence and injustice
  - Consider effects of capitalism and institutions
- Liberation theology's teaching on the 'preferential option for the poor'
  - Gospel demands priority should be given to poor. Christians to show solidarity with poor.
  - Implicaiotns: orthopraxis before orthodoxy

Liberation theology drew on the work of Paulo Freire - who in Pedagogy of the oppressed (1970) invented the term Conscientisation - this is the process by which a person becomes Conscious of the power structure in society. He felt that education would liberate people by raising their consciousness, teaching not only word to read but also the power structure in society. He was opposed to the

143e.

Marx's Teaching on Alienation and Exploitation

Marx taught that alienation occurs when humans are dehumanised and unable to live fulfilling lives. **EXPLOITATION** occurs when humans are treated as objects and used as a means to an end. Note the similarity to Kant's second formulation of the **CATEGORICAL IMPERATIVE** here (treat people not just as a means to an end but always also as an **END** in themselves).

For example, consider a recent purchase from someone you might not know. You might have bought a sandwich from a local supermarket. Did you stop to think about the person serving you at the till? Or, in today's times of 'self-service' – have you thought of the people involved in the building and maintenance of the machines, the famers producing the ingredients needed for the bread and filling of your purchase?

Marx's teaching on **ALIENATION** and exploitation help us to think about the people involved in the **PRODUCTION** of things we value. Marx would say it does matter and should matter that we appreciate the persons involved in the stages of production and do not just see them as a means of production. If we do the latter, we alienate them from society.

Furthermore, technology has revolutionised the world but with the more apparent power we have in this development, the less in control we actually feel. Marx said there is a **HUMAN CAUSE** behind this feeling of powerlessness.

When humans reached the ability to produce **SURPLUS TO REQUIREMENTS**, the favour was granted to those who controlled the means of production and herein beglns class division. This division is evident through the ownership of land, where labour is bought and sold – people are treated as means and not 'ends'. Marx laid the foundations for **SOCIALISM** and

COMMUNISM through his criticism of **CAPITALISM** – the private ownership of land. This private ownership changed the relationship between people and the means of production, leading to the exploitation and alienation of the workers.

What does this look like?

1. FEUDAL LORDS own the land and the means of producing food.

2. SERFS work on the land but don't own it. They rely on feudal lords for access and must give surplus to feudal lords.

3. SUBSERVIENT Serfs alienated from the land on which they work.

This system can be likened to working in a factory. Here, people only understand the part they work on and do not have sight of the whole process. In this way, they are **DEHUMANISED**. The work is necessary as without it, we could not pay for our survival. In this way, exploitation becomes a means to an end. Workers form part of a supply chain and do not know the 'purchasers'.

Neither do those purchasing know the workers - people are **ALIENATED** from their work. Our 'happiness' at cheap prices comes at the expense of other people's happiness - at the expense of the exploitation of others.

Liberation Theology's Use of Marx and Social Sin

Liberation theology began as an **INTELLECTUAL** and **PRACTICAL THEOLOGICAL** movement among those who worked with the poor.

PAULO FREIRE described the process of **'CONSCIENTISATION'** – a process by which someone becomes aware of the power structures in society. **FREIRE**

argued that education should teach people to read the power structures and should work to **TRANSFORM** society and not to just transmit information.

Traditionally, theology had focussed on passing on information. **LIBERATION THEOLOGY** focused on **ACTION** before **EXPLANATION** – **ORTHOPRAXY** before **ORTHODOXY**. Liberation theology became, therefore, a **THEOLOGY OF ACTION**.

Liberation theology proposed that the **KINGDOM OF GOD** is not a place we go to when we die; but is something to work for in this life.

GUSTAVO GUTIÉRREZ, one of the founders of liberation theology, proposed that liberation occurs two-fold:

1. SOCIAL AND ECONOMIC – poverty and oppression are the consequence of human choices and therefore humans can resolve as well. Hence an idea of **SOCIAL SIN**.

2. FROM SIN – to be reconciled with the Divine.

Both 'social and economic' and 'from sin' aspects of liberation must happen together. Gutiérrez claimed that **POLITICAL LIBERATION** is the work of salvation. He emphasised earthly liberation, whereas **JUAN SEGUNDO** emphasised spiritual liberation.

The Bible extracts in the 'key quotations' section allow you to consider how each teaching might have influenced the development of liberation theology. For example, **MATTHEW 25:40** - "whatever you did for one of the least of these brothers and sisters of mine, you did for me" – encourages the **PREFERENTIAL OPTION FOR THE POOR** in the call to side with **'ONE OF THE LEAST'**, i.e. an outcast.

Liberation theology has its origins in 1960s Latin America, a place of corrupt

1964 – Petropolis – Brazil
– looked at poverty in S. America –
– It here a an academic and
practical movement to alleviate
the suffering of the poor.

governments and poverty. Christian groups formed to discuss experiences and practical solutions. Liberation theology therefore became a **THEOLOGY OF HOPE**, with God's love extending both to creation and to liberation.

LATIN AMERICA had found itself at a crossroads, a significant battleground in the cold war conflict between the USA and USSR. Marx had predicted a violent uprising of the oppressed – this seemed to be happening. Liberation theology focused on increasing **HUMAN WELL-BEING** rather than **HUMAN MATERIAL WEALTH**. This links to Marx's understanding that industrialisation can sacrifice the well-being of humans, despite the increase in wealth.

Liberation theology's use of Marx here, seems to be that the process of industrialisation is supported by a structure of sin that then forms part of the organisation of society, and in turn, part of the systems of government and education.

GUTIÉRREZ warned against using every aspect of Marxism but mentions his theories of alienation and exploitation. Gutiérrez also utilises Marx's suggestion that human beings can change the world they inhabit. Gutiérrez considered that people of Latin America wanted to be liberated from capitalism and so he called for the Church to stand with such movements for liberation – **BEING CHRISTIAN NECESSITATES BEING POLITICAL**. Gutiérrez went as far as to say that to not get involved in politics would be equal to helping to keep things the same, even if this situation was wrong/ undesirable.

The **STRUCTURAL SIN** that must be changed can be seen in the injustices experienced by the oppressed. The current social system is one of structural inequality. By failing to address the class struggle, we legitimise the existing system, and in so doing, we act as a part of it. Perhaps Marx's most important contribution to liberation theology is his emphasis on recognising the class struggle against the structures of sin.

The prog. include 2 people who became leading liberation theolgian
Jon Sobrino and Gustavo Guttierez
Jesuit/priest/theolgian.
Peruvian. theolgian/priest.

147

Liberation Theology's Teaching on "Preferential Option for the Poor'

The **GOSPEL** demands that Christians must give priority to the poor and act in **SOLIDARITY** with them. Liberation theology demands we put **ORTHOPRAXIS** before **ORTHODOXY**.

The teaching on **PREFERENTIAL OPTION FOR THE POOR** refers to a **BIBLICAL TREND** to show favour to the oppressed and outcasts. This follows the example set by Jesus – "whatever you did for one of the least of these brothers and sisters of mine, you did for me" **(MATTHEW 25:40).** The phrase was first coined by **FATHER ARRUPE, SUPERIOR GENERAL OF THE JESUITS** in **1968**, and was later picked up by the Catholic bishops of **LATIN AMERICA**. **JUAN SEGUNDO** taught that a preferential option for the poor shows an **AUTHENTIC CHRISTIAN RESPONSE**, avoiding the dangers of neutrality.

JUAN SEGUNDO wrote that the Church "intends to struggle, by her own means, for the defence and advancement of the rights of mankind, especially of the poor". Since we are made in **GOD'S LIKENESS, HUMAN DIGNITY** should be central to what we do. By failing to intervene and by allowing an ongoing social divide, we would prove incompatible with the peace and justice advocated in the Bible.

SEGUNDO differed to **GUTIÉRREZ** because he argued that liberation from sin (**SPIRITUAL LIBERATION**) should come before **SOCIAL LIBERATION**.,as social liberation might not be possible. Even Jesus taught *"the poor you will always have with you, but you will not always have me"* (Matthew 26:11). Segundo still taught we should prioritise the preferential option for the poor - now gained acceptance beyond liberation theology.

JOHN PAUL II used the term in his encyclical **CENTESIMUS ANNUS** (1991). In this, he argued that support of the poor is an opportunity for the moral and cultural growth of humankind. However, this also includes a care for **SPIRITUAL POVERTY** – not just a focus on material wealth:

"This option is not limited to material poverty, since it is well known that there are many other forms of poverty, especially in modern society – not only economic but cultural and spiritual poverty as well". (Centesimus Annus para 43)

This spiritual poverty can be caused by focusing too much on the material goods. **POPE PAUL II** referenced drug and pornography addiction as an indication of a broken social structure. A destructive reading of human needs leaves a spiritual void that is filled by exploitation of the weak. **POPE FRANCIS** encourages the Catholic Church to be a **'POOR CHURCH FOR THE POOR'**.

The **CATHOLIC CHURCH** was concerned about the theological use of Marx as some of Marx's ideas were considered intolerable and thus a danger to use in theology **(CARDINAL RATZINGER)**. Furthermore, Ratzinger (later Pope Benedict XVI) also claimed that using Marx interfered with the **EUCHARISTIC CELEBRATION** of power struggle. Evangelism was in danger of being superseded by violent revolution. Christian liberation should focus on **LIBERATION FROM SIN**, with God being the ultimate liberator. Marxism, Ratzinger claimed, was inherently un-Christian.

BONAVENTURE (1221-74), in **TEMPTATIONS FOR THE THEOLOGY OF LIBERATION (1974)**, criticised liberation theology for prioritising action over the Gospel. He claimed that liberation theology equated theology with politics, and as a result, side-lined Christian evangelism. Bonaventure highlighted that liberation theology focused on structural and not personal sin – despite Jesus' emphasis on **PERSONAL RECONCILIATION** with God.

However, for the starving and oppressed, one can question whether liberation from sin is more important than social liberation. Jesus did teach the importance of inner spiritual change, but he also called for real action – seen in the **PARABLE OF THE SHEEP AND THE GOATS (MATTHEW 25)**. The election of a Latin American Pope might signal the beginning of real impact of liberation theology. Pope Francis named **OSCAR ROMERO** a martyr and asked Gutiérrez to be a keynote speaker at a Vatican event in 2015.

However, in a 2017 visit to **MYANMAR** Pope Francis failed to explicitly denounce the persecution of the **ROHINGYA** Muslims by supposedly pacifist Buddhists.

Confusions to Avoid

1. Liberation theology would claim it is not Marxist, but rather, makes use of Marx's analysis of society. Within liberation theology, Marxism is not treated on its own – it is always considered in relation to the situation of the poor. Marxism is of '**INSTRUMENTAL**' use to liberation theology – an instrument in understanding and responding to the needs of the oppressed. For more on this, read **BOFF** in 'recommended reading'.

2. Christianity would claim that its 'preferential option for the poor' came from the Bible and that Marx's criticism of religion was based on corruptions in which the Church had contributed to oppression.

3. Liberation theology's call for **ORTHOPRAXIS** (living) before orthodoxy (dogma) might imply that the church had not advocated Christian action. This is not true. Christianity had always advocated putting beliefs into practice (see

JAMES "faith without works is dead'). Liberation theology brought to attention the need of religion to affect the whole life – including an active role in the traditionally more secular areas of politics and **ECONOMICS**. This is what made liberation theology distinctive.

Possible Exam Questions

1. To what extent should Christianity engage with atheist secular ideologies?

2. "Liberation theology has not engaged with Marxism fully enough." Discuss.

3. Critically assess the claim that Christianity has tackled social issues more effectively than Marxism.

4. Critically assess the relationship of liberation theology and Marx with particular reference to liberation theology use of Marx to analyse social sin.

Key Quotes

"The growth of the Kingdom is a process which occurs historically in liberation". (Gutiérrez, A Theology of Liberation, 1973, p. 177)

"Then the Lord said to Moses, "Go to Pharaoh and say to him, 'This is what the Lord, the God of the Hebrews, says: "Let my people go, so that they may worship me." (Exodus 9:1).

He has performed mighty deeds with his arm; he has scattered those who are proud in their inmost thoughts. He has brought down rulers from their thrones but has lifted up the humble. He has filled the hungry with good things but has sent the rich away empty. *(Luke 1:51-53)*

"Again I tell you, it is easier for a camel to go through the eye of a needle than for someone who is rich to enter the kingdom of God." (Matthew 19:24).

"The King will reply, 'Truly I tell you, whatever you did for one of the least of these brothers and sisters of mine, you did for me.' (Matthew 25:40).

"For my Father's will is that everyone who looks to the Son and believes in him shall have eternal life, and I will raise them up at the last day." (John 6:40).

"Blessed are the poor in spirit, for theirs is the kingdom of heaven. (Matthew 5:3).

Social division whereby the worker "is depressed...both intellectually and physically, to the level of a machine" (Karl Marx, Early Writings, [1833-4] 1975, p.285

"Education is part of the machine of capitalism and pupils are the cogs in that machine" Libby Ahluwalia and Robert Bowie, Oxford A Level Religious Studies for OCR Year 2, 2017, page 305.

"In Latin America to be Church today means to take a clear position regarding both the present state of social injustice and the revolutionary process which is attempting to abolish that injustice and build a more human order." Gustavo Gutiérrez, A Theology of Liberation, 1974, p. 265;

"It is a will to build a socialist society, more just, more free, and human, and not a society of superficial and false reconciliation and equality." Gustavo Gutiérrez, A Theology of Liberation, 1974, p. 273-412.

"Liberation theology used Marxism purely as an instrument. It does not venerate it as it venerates the gospel". Leonardo Boff and Clodovis Boff, Introducing Liberation Theology, 1987

"Let us recall the fact that atheism and the denial of the human person, his liberty and rights, are at the core of the Marxist theory". Congregation of the Doctrine of the Faith, Instruction on Certain Aspects of the 'Theology of Liberation', 1984, para 7.6

Suggested Reading

Boff, L. and Boff, C. (1987) Introducing Liberation Theology, Burnes and Oates

Gutierrez, G. (1974/2000) A Theology of Liberation, SCM Press, Chapter 4

Congregation of the Doctrine of the Faith (1984) Instruction on certain Aspects of the 'Theology of Liberation'

Wilcockson, M. (2011) Christian Theology, Hodder Education, Chapter 7

Influence of Marx – online resource.
See http://www.philosopherkings.co.uk/Marx.html

Gender and Society

Background

The Christian Church has lagged behind changes in social attitudes (and UK laws) in recent years, particularly on sexual issues such as **CONTRACEPTION**, **ABORTION** and **PRE-MARITAL SEX**, and gender issues such as attitudes to **HOMOSEXUALITY** (including gay marriage). For example, the Church of England still formally disallows homosexual gay partnerships in the **CLERGY** whilst professing to welcome gay church members. Gender issues also include attitudes to **TRANSEXUALS** and the political implications of **FEMINISM**.

Key Terms

- **ESSENTIALIST THEORIES:** Gender is fixed by objective human nature, either by God or by our inherent biology (eg genes)

- **EXISTENTIALIST THEORIES:** Gender is determined by social discourse (Foucault), by upbringing (Freud), or by social conditioning (including religious conditioning)

- **FEMINISM:** A movement and a philosophy emerging form the Enlightenment emphasis on equal rights, but embracing theories of power and social conditioning.

- **SEX:** Refers to the biological and physiological characteristics that define men and women

- **GENDER:** The state of being classified as male or female or transgender (typically used with reference to social and cultural differences rather than biological ones).

- **FALSE CONSCIOUSNESS:** Beliefs and behaviour induced by social attitudes and values which contradict the true interest (economic, political or social) of a person

- **PATRIARCHY:** A system of society or government in which men hold the power and women are largely excluded from it.

- **ETERNAL FEMININE:** Simone de Beauvoir's term to describe the role of woman as some ideal imposed by men (submissive housewife, sex object etc).

Specification

A Level requires us to study the effects of changing views of **GENDER** and gender roles on Christian thought and practice, including:

- Christian teaching on the roles of men and women in the family and society

- Christian responses to contemporary **SECULAR** views about the roles of men and women in the family and society including reference to:

  - **Ephesians 5:22–33**

  - **Mulieris Dignitatem 18–19**

The ways in which Christians have **ADAPTED** and **CHALLENGED** changing attitudes to family and gender, including issues of:

  - motherhood/parenthood

- different types of family (single parent, extended, nuclear etc)

Note: there is not one, but **MANY** Christianities. The specification mentions just one Bible passage of many that need to be taken, and one Roman Catholic Document, Mulieris Dignitatem, in the context of a history of **PAPAL ENCYCLICALS**. Roman Catholics and Evangelical Christians argue against women leadership for different reasons. **QUAKERS** have always espoused strict gender equality and are pacifist.

Gender – Essentialist or Existentialist

ESSENTIALIST gender is essential to biology eg Biblical account of creation "God created them male and female'. Often includes conclusions about roles and/or intelligence eg men are stronger and wiser (**AQUINAS**).

EXISTENTIALIST gender is a product of **CIVILISATION** (de Beauvoir), male expectation, a cultural interpretation of gender roles, or an interpretation of the Bible. E.g. body image is a cultural construction (modern anorexic images very different from Rubens portraits).

Exploitation and Power (Michael Foucault)

The idea that human beings have a **SEXUALITY** is a recent western social phenomenon.

At the start of the 18th century, there was an emergence of "a political, economic, and technical incitement to talk about sex,"with experts speaking about the morality and rationality of sex, fuelled by Catholic teaching on sex, sin and confession" (Foucault).

ENLIGHTENMENT emphasises the empirical nature of sex and gender eg biological differences between men and women, the nature and source of sexual pleasure and supposed **OBJECTIVE** measures of intelligence and emotion

The "world of perversion" that includes the sexuality of children, the mentally ill, and homosexuality all subject to more vigorous prosecution. The labelling of **PERVERSION** conveyed a sense of "pleasure and power" for academics studying sexuality and the 'perverts' themselves.

HYPOCRISY as Middle Class society exhibited "blatant and fragmented perversion," readily engaging in perversion but regulating where it could take place. In 18th century Britain 1 in 5 women were prostitutes – Nelson's mistress Emma **HAMILTON** started out as a 'courtesan'.

The mythical idea that previous generations were **REPRESSED** feeds the modern myth that we now live in a 'garden of earthly delights'. (Foucault)

Culture changes by "interconnected mechanisms" and there has been a proliferation of possible sexualities and forms of **DESIRE**, "a deployment quite independent of the law".

Jimmy **SAVILE** sex abuse scandal (2016) and Harvey **WEINSTEIN**'s alleged abuse of power (2017) illustrate Foucault's argument in 1964 A History of Sexuality, as Foucault argues that power relations define how we see sex and sexuality – the powerful **SUBJUGATE** the weak and convince them of the benefits of compliance (the silence of Weinstein's victims is bought by money, jobs or intimidation).

Roger **SCRUTON** (Sexual Desire, 1986) rejects Foucault's claim that sexual morality is culturally **RELATIVE** and criticises Foucault for assuming that there could be societies in which a "problematisation" of the sexual did not occur.

"No history of thought could show the 'problematisation' of sexual experience to be peculiar to certain specific social formations: it is characteristic of personal experience generally, and therefore of every genuine social order". Roger Scruton, Sexual Desire

The fact that Leviticus chapter 18 defines a **PURITY CODE** which causes to stone to death adulterous women and homosexuals as evil doesn't mean that we don't have our own purity code (for example, found in the extreme disgust of paedophilia – a view different from the Greeks).

Gender as a Fluid Concept – Judith Butler (Gender Trouble 1990)

Christianity has encouraged society to impose a **BINARY** (two-sided) relation of women and men. This is then **IDEALISED** as a **HETEROSEXUA**L form, and in the ideal of a two parent family.

Feminists reject the idea that **BIOLOGY** is **DESTINY** (link this to the **TELEOLOGICAL** view of human identity in Natural Law) , but then develop an account of patriarchal culture which assumed that masculine and feminine genders would inevitably be built up from 'male' and 'female' bodies, making the same destiny just as inescapable.

Butler (1956-) argues (with Simone de Beauvoir) that gender is a **SOCIAL CONSTRUCT**. The idea is not fixed, but fluid. Gender is created by repetition of a type of **BODY LANGUAGE** and social attitudes to rebellion (such as disgust at cross-dressing). With Foucault she sees sex (male, female) as causing gender **STEREOTYPES** (masculine, feminine) which is seen to cause desire (towards the other gender).

'There is no gender identity behind the expressions of gender; ... identity is performatively constituted by the very "expressions" that are said to be its results.' (Judith Butler, Gender Trouble, p. 25)

PERFORMATIVITY of gender is a stylised repetition of acts, an imitation or miming of the dominant **CONVENTIONS** of gender. "The act that one does, the act that one performs is, in a sense, an act that's been going on before one arrived on the scene" (Gender Trouble).

"Gender is an impersonation and becoming gendered involves impersonating an ideal that nobody actually inhabits" (Judith Butler, interview with Liz Kotz in Artforum).

"Performativity has to do with **REPETITION**, very often the repetition of oppressive and painful gender norms" (Judith Butler, Gender Trouble).

Butler calls for **SUBVERSIVE ACTION** in the present: 'gender trouble' -- the mobilisation, subversive confusion, and proliferation of genders -- and therefore identity. She would approve of the transgender movement and its forms of direct action and protest in the UK.

Gender and Women's Liberation

PARADOX in a world of liberation and increased rights we still have the silence surrounding Savile and Weinstein, incidence of domestic and other violence against women, and the continued inequalities in pay and promotion in the workplace. Key dates include:

- **1885** Married women could keep hold of their wealth which previously passed to the husband, so restricting divorce.

- **1864** Contagious Diseases Act reacts to prevalence of venereal disease amongst the armed forces (30%) by permitting "policeman to arrest prostitutes in ports and army towns and bring them in to have compulsory checks for venereal disease. If the women were suffering from sexually transmitted diseases they were placed in a locked hospital until cured". **JOSEPHINE BUTLER** launches protest movement at the labelling and degrading of women.

- **1914-18** Women occupy many men's jobs in armaments factories, but in 1918 Unions insist they are made redundant to make way for returning men.

- **1918** Women over 30 obtain the vote after eight year suffragette struggle.

- **1928** Women over 21 obtain the vote.

- **1960s** the Pill allows women to regulate fertility, (Queen Victoria had eight children) experienced by both upper and lower classes.

- **1967** Abortion Reform Act allows termination up to 28 weeks if certain criteria fulfilled. Mental health criterion easily the most popular.

- **1969** Divorce Reform Act allows divorce for 'irretrievable breakdown' rather than just proof of adultery.

- **2004** Gender Recognition Act allows you to apply for a Gender recognition Certificate and so legally change gender after psychiatric assessment for gender dysphoria.

- **2014** Gay couples can be legally married (but not in church).

- **2017** Church of England issues transgender guidance for its 4,700 schools - "pupils need to be able to play with the many cloaks of identity' and should be able 'to explore the many possibilities of who they might be" including gay, lesbian and transgender. "Transphobic bullying causes damage and leads to mental health disorders", Archbishop of Canterbury.

- **2017** a A Bill to make gender identity a protected characteristic under the Equality Act 2010 in place of gender reassignment and to make associated provision for transgender and other persons halted due to the election.

The Changing idea of Family

Comparing 2005 and 2015, we see a snapshot of a profound change in the concept of family continuing (from nuclear to reconstituted, and from **EXTENDED** to nuclear, and from two parent to one parent and from married to cohabiting).

You don't need to learn detailed statistics for A level.

However it may be worth knowing that the fastest growth has been in **COHABITING** couples followed by **LONE PARENT** families in the decade 2005-15. Married and civil partner families have not grown significantly in the ten year period. However, they are still the largest group overall at 8/19 million (42%). Only around a third of households have two people in them.

So we can say with confidence – families are much less likely to be presided over by a married couple than they were forty years ago – family life is far more **FRAGMENTED** and disparate (lone parent, reconstituted, gay or cohabiting, rather than married). Moreover there are many people of any gender living alone. There may be psychological and social **CONSEQUENCES** of these changes.

From **2014** gay people can legally marry (2% of total) – but overwhelmingly in non-religious services (gay couples can't get married in Church by church law).

Christian views on Gender Roles

Augustine on Gender Roles

In Confessions Augustine list of the qualities of his mother Monica - patience, mildness, obedience, selfless service of others, temperance, piety, and even an aversion to gossip, are **STEREOTYPICAL** feminine virtues and vices.

He also describes his long-term relationship with a **CONCUBINE**. Women have one of two roles – mother or lover. Unlike Aquinas, Augustine sees men and women of equal rational capacity , but women by nature submissive because they are **WEAKER**.

Elaine **PAGEL**'s (1989) analyses of the cultural implications of the doctrine of **ORIGINAL SIN** , especially the role of the story of the Fall in Genesis 3. Pagels lays the blame for Christian sexual repression and misogyny (woman hatred) on Augustine, arguing that Augustine's pessimistic views of sexuality, politics, and human nature would come to dominate in Western culture, and that

"Adam, Eve, and the serpent—our ancestral story— would continue, often in some version of its Augustinian form, to affect our lives to the present day." (Elaine Pagels, Adam, Eve and the Serpent, page 34)

Aquinas on Gender Roles

Aquinas follows **ST PAUL** (*1 Corinthians 11:10 "woman was created for the sake of man"*) in seeing women as **INTELLECTUALLY** inferior. Aquinas sees Ephesians 5:22 "the husband is head of the wife" by virtue of greater intellectual wisdom."Men are wiser and more discerning, and not so quickly taken in", he says.

In attempting to interpret **ARISTOTLE** Aquinas accepts his biological assertion that men are the **ACTIVE AGENT** in reproduction, and women the passive (submissive). It is part of **NATURAL LAW** that women are placed in submission to men – and have to obey men.

Luther (1483-1536) on Gender Roles

The creation of Adam and Eve is God's way of preventing human loneliness (**GENESIS 2**).

Adam and Eve were equals before God, and equally culpable in the **FALL**.

But (like Aquinas) Luther saw men as **SUPERIOR** and more guided by reason and destined to lead in life, and women destined to **SUBMIT**. Women had responsibilities for children and the home. The Lutheran view included equality in principle, but superiority and subordination in practice echoes the contradiction in **ST PAUL** (*Galatians 3:28 'there is neither male nor female'* versus *Ephesians 5:22 "wives submit to your husbands"*).

Luther formulated the doctrine of three estates, which divided society into church, family and state each governed by a **PATRIARCHAL** household as their ideal, i.e. a structure in which the father exercised authority but was also a caring protector. But the **REFORMATION** picture overall is more ambiguous.

MELANCTHON (1497-1560) had theological discussions with highly intelligent women. Luther emphasised that a father performs a Christian act when washing his children's dirty nappies, for example. He also expressed his patriarchal respect for his own wife by calling her Mr Kathy.

Modern church on Gender Roles – Catholic, Liberal Protestant (USA)

The **EPISCOPALIAN** Church of America is the most **LIBERAL** of the Anglican communion of churches. They argue that gender matters because of language, imagery and power relations.

ESCHATOLOGICAL hope is for a future where gender ceases to matter – meantime we make small steps towards **JUSTICE** and **EQUALITY** for women.

"The expression of gender and sexuality are conditioned by culture and by experiences of oppression, especially as racial and ethnic diversity are considered" (Episcopalian Church, USA)

The structures of leadership, the language and the practices need to work together to transform the present.

In the Church of England, women priests were first ordained in **1993** and the first woman Bishop, Libby Lane, consecrated in **2015**. Currently there are 12/78 women Bishops (October 2017).

Christian Views on Social Changes

Linda **WOODHEAD** argues that a gap has opened up between Church Teaching and social attitudes on issues such as contraception and gay marriage. The church, faced with the challenge of **RELATIVISM,** has made increasingly tentative steps towards reform – and in the case of the **CATHOLIC** church, has held steadfastly in public to an orthodox (patriarchal) line.

So the increase in UK citizens identifying as **NO RELIGION** (in 2016 51%) does not equate to a lack of **SPIRITUALITY** but a rejection of orthodox forms of Christianity and the embracing of new forms of spirituality (such as New Age, meditation, mindfulness etc).

The Church of England continues to reject gay marriage in church, whilst taking a contradictory view on homosexual sex – gay priests must be celibate (but often in practice are not) whereas church members generally should be encouraged to be faithful to their partner.

In the Catholic church, research suggest only around 11% of Catholic women in the USA follow the prohibition on contraception and abortion, and 31% are on the pill – so fuelling allegations of **DOUBLE STANDARDS**. Meantime, in Africa **AIDS** infection remains endemic and safe sex officially discouraged by the Church.

CATHOLICS FOR CHOICE argues that "Abstinence before marriage and faithfulness in a marriage is beyond the realm of possibility here. The issue is to protect life. That must be our fundamental goal. African people must use condoms."

Christian Teaching – the Bible

Ephesians 5:22-33

EPHESIANS 5 needs to be interpreted in the context of a revolutionary document presented to a patriarchal culture. *"The apostolic letters are addressed to people living in an environment marked by that same traditional way of thinking and acting". "All the reasons in favour of the "subjection" of woman to man in marriage must be understood in the sense of a "mutual subjection" of both "out of reverence for Christ". Mulieris Dignitatem p 24*

Christian Teaching- Roman Catholic Mulieris Dignitatem (MD)

1971 Pope appoints commission to ensure "effective promotion of the dignity and the responsibility of women" culminates in 1988 in **MULIERIS DIGNITATEM** (of the vocation and dignity of women).

Reaffirms **IDEAL** of Mary as obedient and submissive handmaid of the Lord (Luke1:38), and pure virgin. Like Jesus himself, she is called to **SERVE**. She is the new **EVE** and the prototype of a **NEW CREATION**.

Also confirms the Creation order that "both man and woman are human beings to an equal degree, both are created in God's image". Genesis 1:28

Acknowledges the contradiction between two creation accounts (Genesis 1:28 versus Genesis 2:18-25). MD asserts, against traditional teaching, that

"The biblical text provides sufficient bases for recognising the essential equality of man and woman from the point of view of their humanity". (Mulieris Dignitatem p14)

Word equality here does not mean 'equal rights' to exercise leadership in the church. Interpretation here is **RELATIONAL** and **TRINITARIAN**.

"Man - whether man or woman - is the only being among the creatures of the visible world that God the Creator "has willed for its own sake"; that creature is thus a person. Being a person means striving towards self-realisation (the Council text speaks of self-discovery), which can only be achieved "through a sincere gift of self". (Mulieris Dignitatem p16)

The model for this interpretation of the person is God himself as **TRINITY** (God in Three Persons) as a communion of Persons. To say that man is created in the **IMAGE** and likeness of God means that man is called to exist "for others, to become a gift", (Mulieris Dignitatem).

Affirms the feminine and masculine qualities of God eg "Can a woman forget her sucking child, that she should have no compassion on the son of her womb? Even these may forget, yet I will not forget you". (Isaiah 49:14-15).

The **FALL** 'obscures' and 'diminishes' the image of God but does not eliminate it. But consequences include pain (for women) and death for all. Man also 'shall have **DOMINION** (power) over women" (Genesis 3:16) as a part of the consequences of sin.

However, all 'unjust situations' should be remedied because the fundamental equality of Genesis 2 overrides the effects of the Fall in Genesis 3.

Gender differences need to be preserved as part of the **NATURAL CREATED ORDER**. even the rightful opposition of women to what is expressed in the biblical words "He shall rule over you" (Genesis 3:16) must not under any condition lead to the "masculinisation" of women. In the name of liberation from male "domination", women must not appropriate to themselves male characteristics contrary to their own feminine "originality".

Despite evidence of a new relationship to women reflected in Jesus actions and teachings, and the presence of women as the first witnesses of resurrection , MD reaffirms that

"Virginity and motherhood are two particular dimensions of the fulfilment of the female personality". (Mulieris Dignitatem p 17).

MARY DALY would see the depiction of women as virgin, mother or whore as part of the conditioning of **PATRIARCHY** whereas **DAPHNE HAMPSON** would see the complex interpretations of Mulieris Dignitatem as part of the **IRREDUCIBLY** patriarchal nature of historical Christianity, the Bible and all its interpretations which justify inequality (such as the Catholic teaching against women priests and bishops).

Possible Exam Questions

1. "Christians should resist current secular views of gender" Discuss

2. Evaluate the view that secular views of gender equality have undermined Christian gender roles

3. "Motherhood liberates rather than restricts". Discuss

4. Critically evaluate the view that idea of family is entirely culturally determined.

5. "Christianity follows where culture leads". Discuss

Key Quotes

"One is not born, but rather one becomes a woman.. it is civilisation that produces this creature." Simone de Beauvoir.

"Gender is an impersonation . . . becoming gendered involves impersonating an ideal that nobody actually inhabits." Judith Butler, Gender Trouble

"My argument for the "moral significance" of gender is an extensive attack on the Kantian assumption behind modern feminism—the assumption that what I am essentially is a person, and that persons are essentially genderless." Roger Scruton, Sexual Desire

"According to Scruton's Aristotelian argument, love is to sexual desire as the mature flourishing life of a tree is to the young developing plant". Martha Nussbaum

"There is no gender identity behind the expressions of gender; ... identity is performatively constituted by the very "expressions" that are said to be its results." Judith Butler, Gender Trouble

"Even a pioneering feminist like Germaine Greer is forbidden to speak on campus lest her belief in real and objective sexual differences should threaten vulnerable students who have yet to decide which gender they are". Independent 3.11.17

"Within Christianity, more than in any other religion, women have had a special dignity, of which the New Testament shows us many important aspects." Pope Paul VI

Further Reading

Tong, R. (2013) Feminist Thought, Routledge, Chapter 1

McGrath, A. (2010 5th Edition) A Christian Theology, Wiley-Blackwell, pages 88–89, 336–337

More A. Female Sexuality (Routledge, 2005) synopsis available on peped.org

Messer, N. (2006) SCM Study Guide to Christian Ethics, SCM Press, Chapter 8.

Mulieris Dignitatem, Roman Catholic Encyclical available on peped.org

Pagels, E. Adam, Eve and The Serpent (Vintage, 1989)

Ephesians 5:22–33 peped.org > Philosophy > christian-thought > feminism

Gender and Theology

Background

Paradoxically, Christianity presents itself as a prophetic movement of liberation and belief in a **NEW HEAVEN** and a **NEW EARTH** redeemed by the faithful. Mary **DALY** and Daphne **HAMPSON** are post-Christians feminists who reject the very basis of Christianity and the Christian God-concept. Rosemary **RUETHER** remains a Catholic calling the church to repent and change.

A word of warning though: Christianity isn't one entity and it is dangerous to **GENERALISE**. The **MONTANISTS** of the second to sixth century had women leaders and prophets, and the **QUAKERS** of the past 400 years have always followed a priestless equality where anyone can speak a word from God. Perhaps Christianity (following Emporer **CONSTANTINE**'s conversion in 316) have become too enmeshed in the power structures of many societies to be a prophetic movement and has become a rather laggardly reflection of its times.

Specification

A level requires that we study Ruether's discussion of the maleness of Christ and its implications for salvation including:

- Jesus' challenge to the male **WARRIOR MESSIAH** expectation

- God as the female **WISDOM** principle

- Jesus as the **INCARNATION** of wisdom

Daly's claim that *'if God is male then the male is God' (1996:76)* and its implications for Christianity, including:

- Christianity's 'Unholy Trinity' of rape, genocide and war
  - spirituality experienced through nature

Key terms

- **APOCRYPHA:** That part of the Bible rejected by Protestant Christianity, but containing Wisdom literature which exalts the feminine.

- **ESCHATOLOGY:** The end times, traditionally a time in the future when God judges the world. In feminism, eschatology is realized now with judgement on patriarchy and formation of a new society.

- **FEMINISM:** A movement campaigning for the rights, empowerment and equality of women.

- **GENOCIDE:** The attempt to eliminate a race or a religious group by extreme violence and murder

- **GOD/ESS:** Ruether's genderless term for God

- **HERMENEUTICS:** The study of methods of interpretation and the textual generation of meaning

- **INCARNATION:** Embodiment of some value of goodness or aspect of God

- **MESSIAH:** The 'anointed one' sent by God in fulfilment of Old Testament prophecy to liberate and redeem Israel

- **MONTANISM:** prophetic movement in the second century where women prophesied and claimed visions directly from Christ.

- **PATRIARCHY:** (Two Latin words, pater/arche) rule of the male. A form of society where men dominate, denigrate and oppress women.

- **SEXISM:** Prejudice, stereotyping, or discrimination, typically against women, on the basis of sex.

- **SHEKINAH:** The glory of God which traditionally shone forth from the altar, expelled by patriarchy and rediscovered in the Exodus community of women.

- **SPIRITUALITY:** Response to the metaphysical reality beyond the physical, where the individual forms patterns of self-determination that build the common good.

Structure of Thought - Ruether

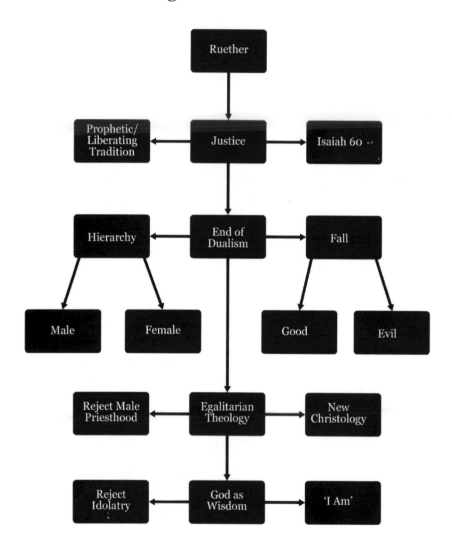

Hermeneutics of Suspicion

Paul **RICOEUR** (1913-2005) asks us to adopt a **HERMENEUTIC OF SUSPICION** when reading a text such as the Bible. We need to be suspicious of the **MOTIVES**, the **VALUES**, the culture of those who wrote it, and not just project our own values onto the text. James O'Donnell comments

"Liberation means, therefore, to opt for the exercise of an ideological suspicion in order to unmask the unconscious ideological structures which dominate and which favour a powerful, privileged minority." (O'Donnell 1982:32)

There is a **WORLD BEHIND** the text (the culture of Jesus' day) and there is a world **IN FRONT** of the text, our own culture. These **TWO HORIZONS** (Gadamer's term) need to merge in a valid interpretation that is **CRITICAL**.

Elizabeth Schüssler **FIORENZA** argues that theology is the product of each writer's experience and that this is determined by the historical and **SOCIAL CONTEXT** of every theologian. Theology is culturally conditioned and shapes, reflects, and serves a particular group's or individual's interests, (Fiorenza 1975:616).

Ruether argues that the Bible is riddled with **PATRIARCHY** and emerged from a world of hierarchy with males in charge. The **FEMININE** is constructed from these patriarchal values.

The social relationships are **ARCHAIC** and inappropriate for our time: they are reflected in a male clergy and a continued tolerance of **INJUSTICE** and **INEQUALITY**.

Behind the interpretation of the Bible lies the acceptance of **ARISTOTLE**'s biology that sees men and women as two separate classes of human and whereby

"The female is not only secondary to the male but lacks full human status in physical strength, moral self-control, and mental capacity. The lesser "nature" thus confirms the female's subjugation to the male as her "natural" place in the universe". (Ruether 1985:65)

Ruether's Hermeneutic

Controlling principle – whatever denigrates women is rejected, whatever builds up and values women is accepted. Then it is **EXPERIENCE** (rather than history) which is the starting-point of theology. The Bible needs to be interpreted anew, and the story of **REDEMPTION** retold in the light of women's experience. This may be linked to the **EXISTENTIAL** theology of Paul **TILLICH**.

There is a **PROPHETIC PRINCIPLE** in the Bible which can be rediscovered and brought to the fore: emphasising **JUSTICE** and the call to be a new people of **LIBERATION**. **ISAIAH 60** gives a radical vision of a just world order.

"God's Shekinah, Holy Wisdom, the Mother-face of God has fled from the high thrones of patriarchy and has gone into exodus with us". Ruether, 1985:87

The counter-culture of early Christianity which emphasised this were suppressed, for example, the female **PROPHETS** Priscilla and Maximilla in **MONTANISM**. Priscilla claimed a night vision in which Christ slept by her side "in the form of woman, clad in a bright garment". She adopted a priestly ministry with direct voices and visions from God. Montanists were persecuted and ultimately suppressed with violence in the sixth century.

SEXISM is a sin against God/ess and against the fundamental golden thread of **JUSTICE** within the Bible.

"The dominant Christian tradition, if corrected by feminism, offers viable categories for interpreting human existence and building redemptive communities" Ruether, 1985:123

Ruether's God-Concept

GOD/ESS is the ground of all being. God is **GENDERLESS** and to turn God into the **MALE** is a form of **IDOLATRY** that serves men's interests.

In the **OLD TESTAMENT, YAHWEH** is the name of God – it means 'no name' or I **AM WHO I AM**.

Patriarchy encourages **HIERARCHY** with the idea of **TRANSCENDENCE**. Ruether emphasises **IMMANENCE** – God as **BEING** within all things.

Ruether sees God as **WISDOM** – the Greek word **LOGOS** and the idea in **WISDOM** literature (the Book of Wisdom is part of the **APOCRYPHA** – not in the Protestant Bible). **GOD/ESS** has sources in **PAGANISM**, and Babylonian **CREATION** myths – but the **MOTHER NATURE** idea was suppressed by the early Church.

LANGUAGE reflects patriarchal values – **FATHER**, Lord, King. "**OUR FATHER…THY KINGDOM COME**".

Can a Male Saviour Save?

Jesus' **GENDER** is irrelevant. Maleness of Christ has no **THEOLOGICAL** significance. The **MESSIAH** is an iconoclastic (idol-smashing) **PROPHET** in the tradition of **ISAIAH** or **AMOS**.

The real Jesus needs to be rediscovered and the Church should **REPENT** and cast off patriarchal values and images. Jesus is the **INCARNATE WISDOM** of God (**LOGOS**, John 1).

Such a rediscovery embraces a new relation to the earth (link with Mary Daly's **GYN/ECOLOGY**). Feminism is, says Daly, **BIOPHILIC** (loves life). This creative thinking creates communities of liberation who engage in play of ideas. Ruether agrees.

The New Age and the Eschatological Community

Does not lie in the future, **ESCHATOLOGICALLY** as in patriarchal ideas – beyond the grave. Link with theological **IMMANENCE** (God is here now, the new community is realised here, now)

It is brought into being now in the **REDEEMED COMMUNITY – REALISED ESCHATOLOGY**.

Ruether believes church can be redeemed by forming new **BASE COMMUNITIES** with **JUSTICE** at their heart. **CLERICALISM** (male priesthood) is a product of patriarchy and should be rejected.

Early Church experiments such as **MONTANISM** (2nd century) had women leaders: in Acts there is a prophetess, and Paul's argument "I do not allow women to have authority in the Church" (1 Corinthians) only makes sense in context of the rise of women **PROPHETS** in Corinth and discord that surrounded it.

Criticisms of Ruether

In a 1986 debate, Daphne Hampson makes three criticisms of Ruether's position (acronym **HIS**).

- **Historical** Roots of Christianity are Sexist. Ruether ignores the historically-entrenched nature of Christianity, which 'necessarily has one foot in the past'. Incarnation means that God became a human being at a particular time, within a patriarchal worldview. That Jesus only chose male apostles may be no accident. Hampson concludes that 'it cannot be the case that God is related in a particular way to a certain history'. Like Daly, Hampson is a post-Christian. Anthony Thiselton agrees:

"Some texts, by their very nature, draw part of their meaning from the actions, history and life with which they are inextricably interwoven";
Thiselton, New Horizons pg 66.

- **Incarnational** Doctrine is sexist. God 'sent his son'. Metaphors for God are male (with a few exceptions that are never developed). God calls Jesus 'My Beloved Son, whom I have chosen,' and asks Jesus' followers to 'listen to him' (Luke 9:35). Christian creeds ask us to affirm belief in "Jesus Christ, his only Son, our Lord'. Lord and Son are both patriarchal images.

- **Symbolic** world is sexist. The revelation of Christ in history is full of patriarchal symbols and messages. The Prodigal Son is having property divided between two men (Luke 15:11-35). The Good Samaritan is a male. When Jesus visits Martha and Mary, Mary is busy cooking and Martha commended for sitting passively at Jesus' feet, (Luke 1:38-42). Women who were Resurrection witnesses were not believed because the testimony of women is unreliable. Moreover, Paul is a Rabbi and retains some of the Levitical symbolic world of Rabbinic Judaism. Hampson points out 'we do not have stories of a man sitting at the feet of a female teacher'. When stories circulate in Corinth of women prophets, Paul seeks to suppress the upsurge by writing two letters to the Corinthians, both against women's liberation, insisting 'women keep silent in church' (1 Corinthians 14:34-5).

Hampson therefore accuses Ruether of misrepresenting the profoundly historical nature of Christian patriarchy, which still affects Christian theology and practice. Hampson is a **POST-CHRISTIAN**, Ruether a Christian **LIBERATION** theologian.

Background - Mary Daly

Mary Daly (1928-2010) was a radical lesbian feminist theologian who taught at **BOSTON COLLEGE**. She almost always refused to let men into her classes, in 1999, a male student sued the school for discrimination. Daly was suspended and ultimately refused to comply. She also stated she found men disruptive. Lawrence Cunningham calls her 'the gold standard of **ABSOLUTE FEMINISM**."

Structure of Thought - Mary Daly

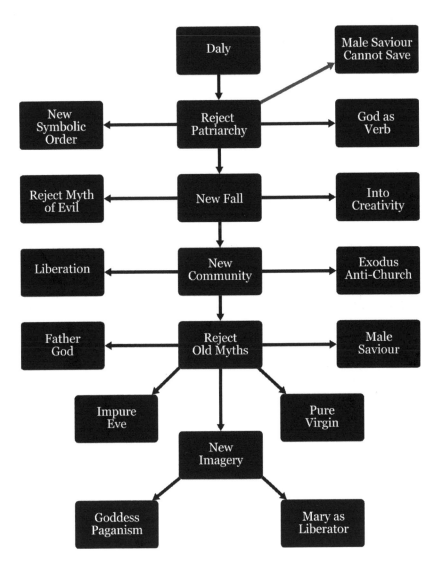

The Myths that Bolster Patriarchy

Daly argues that male **MYTH-MAKERS** constructed an image of the feminine to mould women for their own purposes. The male is the **ROBBER** who robs women of "their myths, their energy, their divinity, their very selves". **PATRIARCHY** has 'stolen our **COSMOS** and turned it into Cosmopolitan magazine" and is the prevailing religion of the entire planet, whose essential message is **NECROPHILIA** (love of **DEATH** eg crucifixion and **MORTIFICATION** - putting our sins to death by self-flagellation).

She calls women to have the courage 'to see and to be' and represent the greatest challenge to the religions of the world. The ultimate **SIN** is patriarchal religion; yet women are **COMPLICIT** by living out the role of the submissive **OTHER**, represented in Christianity as **WEAK, OBEDIENT, DEPRAVED**. As in **AQUINAS'** thought, men are **SUPERIOR, WISE, STRONG, RATIONAL**.

The Patriarchal God

The language of the **FATHER** God legitimates male supremacy and oppression of women – "as God is male the male becomes god".

She rejects the God-image of Christianity in favour of participation in an **ULTIMATE REALITY** - a God-concept 'beyond and beneath'. The **IMAGE** of **GOD** is the creative potential in all human beings. In this **TRANSFORMATION** of symbols of God, God is transformed from a **NOUN** (**FATHER, LORD**) to a verb who is "form-destroying, form-creating, transforming power that makes all things new" (Daly, Beyond God the Father). God is **BEING** and **BECOMING**. We might describe this as a rejection of the Christian God and a rediscovery of earlier feminine god-concepts.

Myth of the Feminine

Daly accuses **AUGUSTINE** and **AQUINAS** of misogyny (women hatred) as they deny women the power to reach their full potential.

The male constructs the feminine as the originator of **EVIL** in the myth of the **FALL** and its interpretations. **EVE** is represented as the **SCAPEGOAT** of male sexual guilt. Daly encourages women to enter a new Fall   - a **FALL** into **FREEDOM**, involving eating the forbidden fruit of **WISDOM** all over again. Two images of women: the **VIRGIN** and the **WHORE**, represented in the image of the **PURE VIRGIN MARY** and the fallen **MARY MAGDALENE**.

- **MARY** = the impossible virgin (still submissive to the will of the Father-God)

- **MARY MAGDALENE** (the fallen woman) = all other women cast in the image of the fallen **EVE**.

Daly calls women to stop playing the role of meek, subservient 'complement' to men, to re-imagine their power and renew the world.

Yet the virgin **MARY** can be adopted by feminism as a symbol of the **AUTONOMOUS** woman, the first woman to fall into **PARADISE**. Mary echoes back to a pre-Christian era of the **GREAT GODDESS**.

The Scapegoat Christ

Daly believes Jesus was simply a limited human being. It is **IDOLATRY** to suggest a **MALE** saviour can represent the eternal **BEING** which is God. Jesus is portrayed by patriarchy as the **SCAPEGOAT** for the sins originating in **EVE**, and the twin idealisations of **CHRIST** and **MARY** have nothing to do with history.

The projection of our evil onto these twin figures of **PURITY** results from an **INABILITY** to accept our own guilt. Feminism rejects the **SCAPEGOAT** Christ with its projections of **VICTIMHOOD** and the worship of the violence of the **CROSS** as part of the **NECROPHILIA** (love of **DEATH**) of patriarchy.

In the development of patriarchy, the male priest becomes the sole mediator controlling access to the deity. Women need to affirm **BIOPHILIA** (love of life).

A Fall into the Sacred

Women in exercising their **FREEDOM** and **POWER** fall into a new sacred space, a **SECOND COMING**, escaping the false **PARADISE** of patriarchal enslavement. They practise **BECOMING** by renouncing the traditional dichotomy of **HETEROSEXUAL/HOMOSEXUAL**, which are patriarchal classifications, to live in an environment that is "beyond, beneath and all around".

Women empowered cut loose from the **PSYCHOSEXUAL** chains that bind them to a patriarchal set of images, and a patriarchal power structure. Women are by nature **ANTI-CHURCH** with its over-emphasis on sexual and gender differences. Women have to 'live now the freedom we are fighting for', and **FEAR** and **GUILT** are no longer used as weapons of oppression. She calls both men and women to leave the church and become "an **EXODUS** community prepared to get on with the business of **LIVING**". Indeed men may understand the manipulation of **POWER** better as they see it from **WITHIN**.

"Male religion entombs women in sepulchres of silence in order to chant its own eternal and dreary dirge to a past that never was". Mary Daly, Beyond God the Father, page 145

Ultimately Daly believes in a new **COSMIC COVENANT** – which renounces the old order of meaningless desires, violence and war.

Gyn/Ecology

Daly plays on words to encourage women to 'weave tapestries of our own kind". She rages against the oppressive system in which "patriarchy is the homeland of males" and where they oppress and demonise women in rites of **SUTTEE** or **WITCH-BURNING**.

She analyses the **LANGUAGE** of patriarchy   and the mind/body/spirit **POLLUTION** this has brought about. **PHALLIC** myths predominate – from the Coca-Cola advert for the **REAL THING** to the Christian hymns glorying in the **DEATH** and real presence of Christ. With spiritual pollution comes pollution of the planet – as the male 'threatens to **TERMINATE** life on the planet through rape (of nature), genocide and war'.

"If life is to survive on this planet, there must be a decontamination of the Earth. I think this will be accompanied by an evolutionary process that will result in a drastic reduction of the population of males." (Gyn/Ecology page 54)

To escape the enslavement and **DENIGRATION** of the male, women need to invent a **NEW LANGUAGE** and set of social relations. Using **CREATIVE ANGER** and **BRILLIANT BRAVERY**, women rediscover 'our **WOMEN-LOVING** love". "We find our original Being and we SPIN our original **INTEGRITY**" and so put **POWER** and **JOY** back into living.

On contraception she comments, showing her playful use of language:

"It is obvious to Hags that few gynaecologists recommend to their heterosexual patients the most foolproof of solutions, namely Misterectomy.

The Spinsters who propose this way by our be-ing, liv-ing, speak-ing can do so with power precisely because we are not preoccupied with ways to get off the heterosexually defined contraceptive dilemma. " (Gyn/Ecology p.239)

Criticisms of Daly

- Black theologian Audre **LOURDE** criticised Daly for refusing to acknowledge the '**HERSTORY** and myth' of women of colour. The severe oppression they have suffered greatly outweighs the discrimination of white women. There's a racial bias to Daly's work and a racist indifference to the plight of minorities who suffer greatest oppression.

- Patriarchy cannot assist in explaining why only a few men in a patriarchy use violence against women and why many males have campaigned for women's rights over the centuries (the first man being Jesus himself who overthrew aspects of anti-women purity code of **LEVITICUS**).

- Daly wanted **WOMEN** to rule men and was herself a lesbian and vegetarian. "I really don't care about men" she commented in an interview. Yet isn't this perpetuating the **DUALISM** she herself rejects as oppressive?

- The **FRAMEWORK** of Patriarchy is assumed in all instances. There is no other explanation given for witch-burning (Christian) or suttee (Hindu). Paradoxically, Enlightenment enquiry provoked an upsurge of interest in alchemy and other forms of magic: it is arguably the flip-side of the stress on autonomous reason. James I wrote a book on witches.

- People who criticise her she calls "**FEMBOTS** doing Daddy's work".

- No analysis of class, wealth or race as instruments of oppression of women.

Confusions to Avoid

1. **Feminists cannot be Christians**. Feminists like Ruether argue that Christianity can be restored to a lost **PROPHETIC** movement, transforming society, but only if patriarchy is rejected. A male saviour is irrelevant to salvation and the male perspective is a gloss overlaying the true gospel, which can be reconstructed as a gospel of liberation and hope. However, both Daphne Hampson and Mary Daly call women out of the church and see Christianity as irredeemably patriarchal. They are post-Christian feminists.

2. **The Church has no response to feminism**. This isn't a fair assessment because the Protestant churches have reformed themselves and allowed women priests and bishops (where appropriate to their order of ministry). The Church of England ordained women **PRIESTS** in 1993 and women **BISHOPS** in 2013. The Roman Catholic Church produced a brave apologetic for its position in not allowing women priests and bishops in Mulieris Dignitatem, which lay great emphasis on the equality of the sexes, but failed to reconcile the **CONTRADICTION** in the Bible between the Paul of Galatians (there is neither male nor female) and the Paul of Ephesians and Corinthians (wives obey your husbands, and "I do not allow women to have authority over a man'). Moreover, the Catholic persistence in advocating the **RHYTHM** method of contraception suggests that the **AUTONOMY** of women and their right to choose is still being overridden by the male perspective.

3. **A male saviour cannot save**. This extreme position, taken by Mary Daly, would appear to overlook the revolutionary attitude of Jesus towards women whom he included in his inner circle and addressed as equals –

"daughter, your faith has made you well, go in peace" (Mark 5). Arguably when Jesus 'emptied himself taking the form of a servant' (Philippians 2:7), he also gave up the genderless **INFINITY** of God (Yahweh – means 'I am who I am'). God cannot have a gender and so if Jesus is one with God his gender must be irrelevant for salvation. Messiah is a genderless idea. Emphasis on the gender of Christ and the virginity of Mary comes later as the male-dominated church hierarchy produces creeds which impose uniformity on belief and cast out so-called heretics, such as the **MONTANISTS**.

Possible Exam Questions

1. 'A male saviour cannot save'. Discuss with reference to the theologies of Rosemary Ruether and Mary Daly.

2. "If God is male the male is God'. Discuss

3. Critically contrast the theologies of Ruether and Daly.

4. "The Church is irrevocably patriarchal'. Discuss

5. "God is genderless, and so the idea of the Father-God is idolatry". Discuss

6. "Only a spirituality of women can save the planet from environmental degradation and war'. Discuss

Key Quotes

"If God is male then the male is God' Mary Daly (1996:76)

"It is obvious to Hags that few gynaecologists recommend to their heterosexual patients the most foolproof of solutions, namely Misterectomy". Mary Daly (Gyn/Ecology p239)

"The dominant Christian tradition, if corrected by feminism, offers viable categories for interpreting human existence and building redemptive communities". Rosemary Ruether, 1985:123

"Some texts, by their very nature, draw part of their meaning from the actions, history and life with which they are inextricably interwoven". Anthony Thiselton, New Horizons pg 66.

"The female is not only secondary to the male but lacks full human status in physical strength, moral self-control, and mental capacity. The lesser "nature" thus confirms the female's subjugation to the male as her "natural" place in the universe". Rosemary Ruether (1985:65)

Reading

Listen to Mary Daly interview
https://archive.org/details/KDVS_The_Fringe_4-5-06

Mary Daly, Beyond God the Father, (Beacon, 1992)

Mary Daly, Can a Male Saviour Save? (Select 'Extracts' from:
http://peped.org/philosophicalinvestigations/christian-thought/feminism/)

Elisabeth Schussler Fiorenza, Sharing Her Word (T & T Clarke, 1998)

Daphne Hampson, After Christianity (SCM, 2002)

Rosemary Ruether, Sexism and God-talk (Beacon, 1993)

Bible Passages such as 2 Corinthians 11:3 and 1 Tim 2:14 became the argument for the subordination of women, and Mark 5 and John 8 for Jesus' more liberating attitudes to women. Isaiah 60 gives the prophetic call for justice. Paul in Galatians 3:16 seems to contradict Ephesians 5. Can they be reconciled?

Hampson, (After Christianity, 2002), states that if Christianity is true, God cannot be thought of as moral or good "given the harm that this myth has done to women" (Hampson 2002: xv). The Christian myth is misogynistic (Hampson 2002: xvi) and morally suspect (Hampson 2002: vxiii).

Revision Access

Opening March 25th 2018

Our unique guides provide you with a special benefit - your own revision site which is fully integrated with the guides and only available to purchasers.

All our revision materials for Christian Thought, Ethics, and Philosophy of Religion are available to each purchaser of any individual guide. Resources include model essay samples found at the back of each chapter, and also:

- Articles
- Extracts
- Handouts
- Roadmap
- Summary
- Videos
- Whizz Through Powerpoints

Visit: peped.org/revision-access

Postscript

Peter Baron read Politics, Philosophy and Economics at New College, Oxford and afterwards obtained an MLitt for a research degree in Hermeneutics at Newcastle University. He qualified as an Economics teacher in 1982, and taught ethics at Wells Cathedral School in Somerset from 2006-2012. He is currently a freelance writer and speaker.

Daniella Dunsmore trained in Theology at Cambridge University. She is currently subject leader in Religious Studies at Thetford Grammar School, speaks at Conferences, and is a Teach First Ambassador.

In 2007 we set up a philosophy and ethics community dedicated to enlarging the teaching of philosophy in schools by applying the theory of multiple intelligences to the analysis of philosophical and ethical problems. So far over 700 schools have joined the community and over 30,000 individuals use his website every month.

To join the community please register your interest by filling in your details on the form on the website. We welcome contributions and suggestions so that our community continues to flourish and expand.

www.peped.org contains **EXTRACTS** and **FURTHER READING** mentioned in the exam specification, plus additional articles, handouts and essay plans. Notice that the exam specification merely gives guidance as to further reading - you may use any source or philosopher you find relevant to the construction of your argument. Indeed, if you have the courage to abandon the selection (and any examples) introduced by your textbook, you will relieve the examiner of boredom and arguably launch yourself on an A grade trajectory.

30233818R00107

Printed in Great Britain
by Amazon